SCIENCE
of
ASCENSION

A STUDY OF THE ABSOLUTE

Other Writings by Lillian DeWaters

All Things Are Yours ◆ The Atomic Age
The Christ Within ◆ The Finished Kingdom
Gems ◆ God Is All
The Great Answer ◆ Greater Works
I Am That I Am ◆ In His Name
The Kingdom Within
Light ◆ Light of the Eternal
Loving Your Problem ◆ The Narrow Way
The One ◆ Our Sufficient Guide
Our Victory ◆ Practical Demonstration
The Price of Glory ◆ Private Lessons
The Seamless Robe ◆ The Time Is at Hand
The Understanding Series
The Voice of Revelation ◆ Who Am I
Word Made Flesh

Available through:
Mystics of the World
Eliot, Maine
www.mysticsoftheworld.com

SCIENCE
of
ASCENSION

A STUDY OF THE ABSOLUTE

Lillian DeWaters

Arise, shine; thy light is come;
the glory of the Lord is upon thee.
— Isaiah 60:1

SCIENCE OF ASCENSION

Mystics of the World First Edition 2014

ISBN-13: 978-0692278734
ISBN-10: 0692278737

Published by Mystics of the World, Eliot, Maine
www.mysticsoftheworld.com

Cover graphics by Margra Muirhead
Printed by CreateSpace
Available from Mystics of the World and Amazon.com

 formats

DeWaters, Lillian, 1883 – 1964
Originally published:
Lillian DeWaters Publications
Stamford, Connecticut, 1929

Contents

PREFACE 7

CHAPTER I
    LABORLESS DELIVERANCE 11

CHAPTER II
    IS MAN GOD? 23

CHAPTER III
    THE SCIENCE OF OUR BEING 45

CHAPTER IV
    PRACTICAL DEMONSTRATION 63

CHAPTER V
    RIGHT INTERPRETATION 83

CHAPTER VI
    PARADISE.. 104

CHAPTER VII
    ROLL AWAY THE STONE 117

ABOUT THE AUTHOR 142

*To Those Who Would
Know and Practice Identity*

Preface

Books, teachers, instruction, presenting the kingdom of heaven within and at hand, are spiritual lamps lighting everyone who presents himself a willing disciple.

Every advancing period delivers a clearer and more practical view of perfect Life and Its perfect expression. As ideas of God, self, universe advance to truer conceptions, thought gently rises from the material basis to the true understanding of being.

Absolute Science reveals the truth of individual identity, and this revelation is the light which "shineth in darkness and the darkness apprehendeth it not."

If one knows not his own identity, is it to be wondered that he wanders about as in a dream? How can one demonstrate his perfect, immortal identity unless he accepts and understands it?

Absolute Science presents the way of perfect being and perfect universe at hand, and from this point it demonstrates its power, dominion, and authority. Waking to the true consciousness of one's being as Spirit, one automatically breaks the yoke of bondage and rises to divine heights.

For those ready and willing to listen and be shown the Science of Ascension, the way is big with blessings. How can one gain a richer and more practical understanding of life except by gaining richer and fuller insight of his own being? "What thou seest, that thou be-est," said one with right vision.

Many seem slow to accept advanced ideas and so come to a standstill in understanding and in demonstration. Truth demands that we advance in the spiritual apprehension, understanding, and demonstration of Reality as the only fact of existence. The hour strikes for *each* to demonstrate self-knowledge and self-government. The commands of spiritual sense when recognized and fulfilled lead to the illumination of spiritual understanding, restoring the lost sense of one's perfection and revealing *one* God, *one* Christ, *one* universe, *here and now.*

The glories of revelation await him who, viewing the ascended Christ, accepts this Christ as his own Selfhood.

"Who did hinder you, that ye should not obey the truth?" (Gal. 5:7). Why give power to physical personality, to man-made creeds and laws hindering the glorious sense of individual freedom, power, and authority?

Perceiving and obeying the light of impersonal Christ, one makes rapid progress in the practice of truth and in the overcoming of the false beliefs called sin, sickness, and bondage.

Jesus preached Truth, presenting a way of deliverance from suffering and limitation. Spiritual seers since that period have spiritually interpreted his message, bringing it more clearly to individual and universal recognition and understanding. Truth having been revealed, it needs now to be intelligently understood and practiced.

The significance in which one interprets perfect identity, perfect embodiment, and perfect universe determines for him his advancement in individual, spiritual demonstration. In proportion as one perceives and accepts the truth that he is Spirit—limitless, boundless, lawless—is he prepared to view the glories awaiting his vision.

Learning the power of Soul over sense and Science over belief, we find demonstration easy and natural, and this new birth delivers to us ineffable joy, peace, and harmony. As sense is uplifted to receive, retain, and practice Reality, we are redeemed from erring manifestation, and we reach the fruition of the promise: "If ye abide in me, and my words abide in you, ye shall ask what ye will, and it shall be done unto you."

What "stone" or obstacle can withstand Omnipotence? When one has the living Fire, he fears nothing, for this living Flame is a law unto Itself and is absolute authority.

—Lillian DeWaters

Chapter I

LABORLESS DELIVERANCE

Jesus prophesied that a vision greater than healing the sick, greater even than raising the dead, should sometime descend upon us.

Does not vision delivering cessation of sin and sickness transcend vision of healing? And would not immunity from death transcend raising the dead?

Jesus practiced and taught a Science which enabled him not only to help and bless others on their plane of experience, but which lifted himself into a realm or state of consciousness called *ascension*.

Ascension is the door opening to us a new heaven and a new earth. In this perception of Being we find our immaculate immortality and our transcending glory.

There is a laborless way in which one may leave undesirable earthly conditions. This way is a state of consciousness *wherein such conditions cannot exist.*

If one reports that his body is sick, that his purse is empty, that his mind is sorrowful, the Christ is saying unto him, "The kingdom of perfect Life is within you. In the kingdom are many mansions. Arise! Enter! Behold!"

Here, the notion that one should combat undesirable conditions or that one should heal undesirable conditions is laid aside for vision of a higher order. For illustration, let us suppose that upon entering a house, one chooses to live in the kitchen. The house has many desirable rooms, but in this kitchen he finds himself confronted with dishes, brooms, and labor, and he finds that he must deal with them. Thus, his experience becomes unhappy and distasteful.

But why attack brooms and dishes as though they were opposing oneself? Are there not other rooms in which one may live, automatically dispensing with kitchen labor?

One finds instant and tremendous relief in his mind when he perceives that he need not attack so-called external experience. Rising into a higher realm of thought, one automatically transcends undesirable conditions. As individual consciousness is uplifted, conditions simultaneously take on a new aspect. One's whole universe is transformed for him as he ascends in consciousness.

We escape the condition called disease as we perceive and understand that we are immutable Life. We put off limitation and bondage as we accept and practice our Reality. Remaining in the library, one laborlessly escapes the toils of the kitchen; and entering that realm of consciousness which perceives with Jesus, "Ye are the light," one laborlessly puts off darkness.

As the student instructed in music avoids discords by beholding and understanding harmony, so do we overcome and avoid discordant conditions by beholding and claiming our primitive state of perfect being.

If one considers himself a material being, he labors with material limitations. If one considers himself a mental being, he labors with mental limitations. But should one cease the belief that he is material, cease also the belief that he is mental, and enter that realm of consciousness wherein he perceives that he is God-being, spontaneously he leaves the so-called physical and mental states and enters the state of Spirit.

One finds it utterly impossible to formulate a belief that Spirit can be sick, that Truth can be untrue, that Intelligence can be ignorant. Therefore we open our vision that our King of Glory may appear.

Since we know in our heart that there are no false conditions in Spirit, then our escape from false conditions is to *be* Spirit!

"I say unto thee, Arise," is not spoken to the so-called dead, but to the living.

As ignorance is overcome by intelligence, so human sense is overcome by spiritual consciousness.

The day of attempting to heal so-called conditions is drawing to a close. There is being ushered into view a higher vision—the Science of Ascension; the Science of *being* the Truth; the Science of *spontaneously* experiencing health and blessedness.

With the coming of the automobile, the use of the horse began to diminish. With the coming of the radio, the use of the victrola lessened. With the coming of the perception that we are Spirit, the conditions called sickness, sin, and death begin to vanish.

Wings are not given a butterfly by the cutting off of feet, nor does one receive heavenly harmony by cutting down or attacking his experience and environment. Not by might, but by spiritual perception, saith our Lord-Self.

This glorifying vision—that *we* are the being of Truth—is our new and immortal birth, and in light such as this we perceive our actual being.

Spiritual awakening, or awakening to Self as Spirit, is the uplifting of individual consciousness into eternal Truth. Perceiving that there is nothing external to combat, heal, or destroy, one makes rapid strides in individual spiritual advancement; and what is called inharmony, transformed by the higher vision, disappears.

Truth awakens us to receive spiritual realities. Truth calls us to hear wondrous ideas. With the coming of illumination, the dream of material

14

existence is dispelled. As light (understanding) appears, darkness (unenlightenment) vanishes. As Christ, our real Self, appears to us, unreality or inharmony disappears.

> "As a vesture shalt thou change them ... In the twinkling of an eye, we shall be changed."

Thought and vision becoming exalted, no longer does one put new wine into old bottles or patch discordant bodies with right ideas. Wings are not placed upon a caterpillar, nor should one attempt to place a body "white as light" upon a body that is considered mortal and structural.

The immaculate spiritual body (the temple of our Lord) awaits our claim and our laborless acceptance. Jesus assured us that his vision reported the perfect universe at hand, the white fields harvested, and the radiant body prepared.

> "Eye [material vision] hath not seen the things which God hath prepared for him ... His going forth is prepared as the morning ... Inherit the kingdom prepared for you ... Thou preparest a table before me."

Recognition and acceptance of our God-being enables us to perceive abundance, happiness, and harmony prepared and at hand. As our immortality becomes apparent to us, the body responds to our ascending vision. Such transfiguration is the spontaneous shadowing forth of the new and glorified state of consciousness.

15

The Science of Ascension, revealing to us that we are Soul, seizes and holds our vision, and human beliefs and limitations cease proportionately. *Come up higher!* This is the call of the One. Come up into a higher perception and here experience illumination and transfiguration.

"He made darkness his secret place ... The darkness and the light are both alike to thee."

No matter how great may seem one's mental darkness, there is hidden in him the glory of his Lord. The message that we are Life, Truth, and Love is the Light that shineth eternally in us, though we may comprehend It not. Because of this ever-present and transcending Light, one is always delivered, potentially, and no dream ever takes from him his changeless, ever-present glory and immortality.

Since one is *now* a perfect and immortal being, why speak or write at all about redemption, resurrection, and ascension? The answer is obvious. If one knew and had demonstrated his redemption, resurrection, and ascension, he would not be present to ask this question. His body would disappear from material sight and would be deathless.

Jesus Christ presented to us all the way of salvation from false belief—belief in the reality of material limitation and bondage. Material sense of life must be put off, and false belief must yield to truth, for, "In Christ shall all be made alive." As one apprehends and retains the correct view of ideal being—perfect, unfallen, changeless identity—the untrue sense of life is *laborlessly* put off and vanquished.

As the Science of Being dawns upon us, we relinquish untrue beliefs for spiritual realization, establishing in this dream of material existence our understanding of truth.

"Ye shall know the truth." —Jesus

We gain the control of Soul over sense in the very way that Jesus taught and demonstrated. In proportion as the truth of Jesus' life and teaching is apprehended and demonstrated by the individual does the individual "put on," or experience, his harmonious, individual identity.

One solves a problem in mathematics understanding that the correct answer already exists, and this perception also applies to the solution of the problem of so-called material existence. The answer is prepared, established from eternity, and individually one obtains, retains, and practices the Science of Being.

"When this mortal shall have put on immortality, then shalt be brought to pass the saying that is written, Death is swallowed up in victory." —Paul

True being is not lost, fallen, or resurrected, and the kingdom of eternal harmony remains

17

forever omnipresent in Consciousness. Transition from an untrue sense of life to a new and true sense constitutes resurrection.

Being cannot be transformed, for the reason that being is changeless and immortal. It is wrong *belief* or mistaken *sense* which must yield to the harmony of spiritual sense, or to the Science of Ascension.

Although individual spiritual identity is actually immortal, perfect, and complete and not imperfect, human, and mortal, nevertheless, the *perception* of this fact seems to dawn upon one by degrees. Spiritual understanding is perceived and demonstrated by the individual gradually and gently, culminating in the divine requirement, "Be ye therefore perfect."

Our individual demonstration of spiritual power over false sense becomes evident only as we rise to our nativity in Spirit. One emerges step by step from the belief that he is material and mortal to the recognition that he is Spirit and that all his experience is spiritual. A metaphysical teacher wrote: "Emerge gently from matter into Spirit."

We wait expectantly, and finally the child disappears and the man takes his place; yet the man is always here potentially and actually. We discern and perceive Truth spiritually, and finally the unreal (sense) disappears and the real state is enthroned. Perfect being is always here inherently and eternally.

With the disappearance of the caterpillar, the crawling motion is gone automatically; the butterfly does not crawl. With the disappearance of the mortal (untrue belief), the sick and dying habits are gone. Immortal being is not sick or sinful. With the acceptance in individual consciousness of the perfect, changeless state, the untrue expression ceases automatically.

"Overcome evil with good." Overcome the belief of mortality with the realization of immortality. Overcome the belief of sick, discordant body with the conviction of perfect and changeless body. Overcome the unawakened state of consciousness with the living fire of insight and perception.

> "The law of the Spirit of life in Christ Jesus hath made me free from the law of sin and death." —Paul

Immortal being is not bound by fetters or hampered by dreams. Immortal being is free Spirit—omnipresent, omniscient, and omnipotent. Let this be our vision.

The putting on of immortality is the *awakening* to the fact that a spiritual being is perfect and that there is no other being!

Nothing opposed to Reality can ever actually exist. Opposition and separation appear only to dull eyes and dim vision. Perfect being never changes, no matter what may be one's viewpoint. As the individual harmonizes his vision with Reality, he laborlessly experiences peace, power, glory, and immortality.

"The light shineth in darkness; and the darkness comprehendeth it not." —John

As the light shineth in darkness, so health shineth in one who reports sickness; and in him who declares that two and two are five, there still abides consciousness of the fact that two and two are four. Thus our infinite Self supplies all our needs, fulfills all our desires, and delivers all our ideals.

Truth, true and ideal being, is here without beginning and without ending. Individual sense, however, perceives, accepts, and demonstrates *the full dominion of Spirit,* according to individual faith, vision, and understanding.

One's life is not here in a coming state, but his life is here in a perfect and complete state. The same thing may be said of individual embodiment. It rests with us each to perceive and demonstrate this eternal fact of being.

"Be ye reconciled to God" is scriptural advice. Let us reconcile ourselves to the fact that we are dealing with one Substance only. Vision such as this quickly clears away the cloud, quickens the faith, and brings one face-to-face with his reality.

Jesus showed us the pathway leading from the state called mortality (human sense) to the actual state of immortality (Spirit). He portrayed to us how the dream of material existence may be broken, how dream laws may be set aside, and how sickness, disease, sin, and death may be *laborlessly* annihilated.

It has been scientifically stated that either by suffering or by Science one comes to himself—one arrives at the point, "Be ye therefore perfect."

"Ye shall know the truth," declared Jesus. We are not required to "know the truth" *after* we have regained our perfect state (returned to our Father's home), but *now,* in the dream of material existence, is the time and place for us to discern and experience the Truth that delivers us to freedom.

This Truth may become known to us individually, either through suffering—the overcoming, step by step, of false sense with true ideas—or through Science of Ascension.

There is a way *above* the taking of human steps, above suffering, above climbing and laboring. This way is the Science of Ascension, the Science of Fulfillment, the Science of, "the last shall be first," the Science of, "fields white already to harvest."

In our everyday experience we see ways of traveling from one geographical place to another. One may walk over the distance; he may motor, or he may travel by airplane. But if he could bridge that distance by *being there* without any process of traveling or "going," this deliverance would illustrate the Science of Ascension.

The prodigal son was confronted with the problem of regaining his perfect state of being. So are we. If in the attempt to return, one takes the mental position of climbing, overcoming, laboring, this process is what has been termed the way of "suffering," for here one is supposed to learn Truth through experience, and this entails constant effort, practice, and labor.

If, however, one glimpses the fact that he has *never left* his perfect kingdom, then he sees that he is not required to return; he is required only to know that he has never wandered away but in a dream, and that he is now and here, uninterruptedly and unchangingly, a perfect being of Life, Truth, and Love.

This is laborless deliverance. This is not the Science of moving up and on, but the Science of remaining still; not the Science of putting on or putting off experience, but the Science of recognizing and accepting Reality.

The Science of Ascension is the Science of *laborless deliverance,* the Science of seeing face-to-face, the Science of *experiencing* Reality.

Chapter II

IS MAN GOD?

To announce that *we are Spirit* means that we recognize and accept Spirit, God, as our reality and as our true Self.

Many have refrained from accepting the wonderful vision that we are Life, Truth, and Love because of the boldness of the statement. But when this fact is stated in another way, when it is couched in different phraseology, one readily confirms and sanctions it.

Let us be big enough in vision and great enough in nature to recognize and accept truth, no matter who states it or in what raiment of words it be clothed. One of insight penetrates the garment of language and knows that the leaven is working, no matter how many measures of meal may seem to conceal it.

Suppose we are asked the current metaphysical query: "Is man God?" What is our reply?

Our reply is this: the question cannot be intelligently answered as it stands, for the reason that the words *God* and *man* are open to many different interpretations. But if one pierces the wall of ambiguity and, discerning the underlying meaning, asks the question in more precise language, it can be satisfactorily answered.

Let the question be stated: "Are we Life, Truth, and Love?" This language is understood and does not need interpretation as though it were a foreign tongue.

When one hears the word *man,* immediately the mind questions, "Does this mean the real or the false man? Does this question refer to the mentality, the Soul, or the body?" If, therefore, students, teachers, and writers avoid using the word *man* and substitute a word which is common and easily understood, much confusion occurring in metaphysical teaching will be eliminated.

The same misunderstanding occurs with the word *God.* Here one spiritually unenlightened may regard *God* in a personal sense. We therefore use the words *Truth, Spirit, Soul, Reality,* etc. to bring the light more clearly to individual consciousness.

Writers of the Bible, as well as some well-known metaphysical writers of recent times, speak of man as "image," "expression," "manifestation," "idea." Can it be that this image means you and me—the individual himself? Can it be that I myself am an image, an expression, a manifestation only?

Verily, no. There is no one but whom, as soon as he receives a certain baptism of the fire of insight, chafes under the notion that he himself is an "image." There is something in him which whispers to him that he is greater than an image, greater than a manifestation or an idea. If he penetrates a little more deeply, if he opens his vision a little more fully, he soon perceives just what it is that is the image and just what it is that is called man, the image of God.

It is the body that is the image. The body is the manifestation or expression of individual consciousness. The body images, enacts, portrays, expresses, manifests the health, life, strength, power, intelligence, substance, and reality of individual consciousness.

Perceiving that man is the body, or embodiment, one can then clearly accept that God (invisible Life) is not man (visible body), nor is man (visible body) God—*yet they are one and inseparable.*

One would not say that the person outside the mirror is the form in the mirror. The person outside is not an image or expression, but the form in the mirror is the expression of that form standing before the mirror. One is not the other; still they are one, and they are inseparable.

Thus if one questions, "Is man God?" the answer is, "Man, or image, is not God, or Substance; but they are one as Intelligence and idea, Manifestor and manifestation, Soul and embodiment."

Individual body (man, or manifestation) is the activity, expression, and manifestation of individual self.

We do not consider Self a picture or an idea or a manifestation. Such belief would not agree and coincide with our living Teacher, who says throughout all ages, times, and discoveries, "I am the life. I am the truth. I am the way!"

Individual being, or the *being* of the individual, is the one Life, Intelligence, and Substance. There is only one Being, and this One is All. We cannot have being outside this One. All being is Christ, God. All life is Reality, God. All intelligence is Truth, God.

Have no fear in stepping out upon the waves of new ideas and in claiming the glory of your immaculate being. Individual being comprises both Consciousness and body, both Life and Its expression, for they are *one and inseparable.* To consider oneself manifestation only, is to fear to step out upon the great sea of understanding.

Everything that is real, that is true, that is perfect is included in the One. The One is Universal (Father) and individual (Son)—*one* being. The reality of the individual Self can be nothing else than the one Reality, *for there is nothing else to be.*

One can easily perceive that all nature symbolizes that the son is a son for a time, until finally he "puts on," or becomes, a father. In the beginning of our metaphysical study we would no doubt have been startled had we been informed of the majesty and the omnipotence of our being. However, we found it easy to be children of God, sons and daughters of God, manifestations and ideas of God. But hearts now leap to the music of the fuller vision, and exaltedly one receives the new name in his forehead.

How could Intelligence and Its idea be divided? How could Soul and Its embodiment be separated? Nay, it cannot be. Life, Being, is One, and this One is *all-inclusive*. The universe, including man (body of the individual), is the body of Truth, God.

> "Thine eyes did see my substance, and all my members were fashioned when as yet there were none of them." —David

The real body, the perfect body, the divine body, is the manifestation of Wisdom, Intelligence, Life, Substance, Being, and it is this perfect, immaculate body that is called man—the image of God.

Let us claim the highest; so shall the Highest claim us. It has been said by men of wisdom that as one approaches Truth, so does Truth approach him. If one feels that he must not hope for or expect too much, that it might be safer to be son than Father, let him consider such scriptural advice as this:

> "Let us come boldly to the throne of grace ... Great is thy boldness of speech ... Ye are the light of the world ... Let your light shine ... Fear not! No man may say that Jesus is the Lord, but by the Holy Ghost."

Thus, we are both Creator and creation; both Intelligence and idea; both Soul and body. And this unit is *indivisible, inseparable, irresistible, everlasting,* and *eternal.*

It is curious that an understanding of the body is one of the last revelations to come to many, yet one of the first questions that a student asks. The thought of the body seems often to tear one asunder.

Now, many of us have discovered that we do not understand a thing until we are in a position to understand it. That is, we may hear or read a right answer to a question, yet our ears and eyes are dull and blinded, and often the meaning escapes us. Years later, perhaps, the right answer presents itself again, and now how differently it appears to us. We hail it with great joy. The answer is always here, but one perceives Truth according to his individual receptivity.

When one takes ownership of his body, as though his body were *outside* his consciousness, he feels a responsibility, and very often a heavy one. If, for instance, the body seems weak and sick, his belief may be that it should be fixed up so that it will look right and act right again. By assuming personal ownership over his body, he automatically assumes responsibility and makes himself *personally* accountable for the health, harmony, and maintenance of his body. Is this not so?

Shall we then stop feeding the body, clothing the body, caring for the body? Not at all. But we can *change our perception of body.* We can come into a higher understanding of body and automatically bless not only our bodies and ourselves, but bless the whole world.

Yea, Self does not have a body of destructible flesh and bones—a body subject to age, limitation, and disease. Do you suppose that a spiritual being could be weak and weary, old and crippled? Unthinkable!

Do you recall how Jesus brought attention to the growing of the lily? How beautiful its body! How fragrant its perfume! How irresistible its form! Yet how wholly *unconscious* of its body. Jesus, discerning our need, said, "Consider the lily; it assumes no responsibility, yet behold its beauty of form and its radiance of being." And you, do you not know that infinite Reality places you in a far higher position than this lily growing in the field? Is it not to be expected that you have a form and a body superior to that of a simple flower growing in the earth?

Sitting under a great shade tree one day, listening to the carol of the birds and the hum of the bees, it came to a thoughtful person how much more he would enjoy nature at that moment were he not fatigued. There seemed a sense of unrest in his body. Quite naturally, he carried on a conversation with his inner self about it.

"Life would be so much more delightful," he meditated, "if people were never sick, if the body were not subject to disasters, discords, limitations. Of course, there isn't really any such body, but there seems ...."

"Well, why should you think about your body?" came back the answer.

"Yes," he thought, "that's it. Why should I be *compelled* to think of it? I really know so little about the body anyhow. I do not understand how I live or how I sleep in the body. I do not understand how my blood circulates or how my food digests. In fact, now that I see it, I know little or nothing about the body as far as the substance or the reality of it is concerned."

"Well, then why have any unnecessary care or worry over it at all? Can there be any body except the body of Truth? Is there anything besides Truth?" questioned the voice.

"What a wonderful thought!" he mused. "To be sure, Truth is my consciousness, and why shouldn't Truth be my body as well? Am I consciousness *and* body?"

"You are not dual," came the answer. "You are one. Whatever there is of you must be the *All* of you. You are Myself. *I* am Yourself. Your body is Mine. My body is Yours. This is one Whole, one *All*, one Being, one action, one form, one Life, and one embodiment of this Life."

Unconsciously he had been caught up by Spirit, and now simultaneously there came to him an illumined sense of joy, uplift, and harmony.

Have we not all noticed that when the body is perfectly well and normal that it causes us no concern—in fact, we quite forget it for the time? We have it, of course, but it is much the same as a shadow; it goes along with us wherever we wish to go, but we have no anxious concern about it, and at times we are altogether unconscious of it.

Turn now to a consideration of the night dream. You dream, for instance, that you are traveling with a party of friends in an ocean liner. You plainly see the great ship; you watch the white waves; you look upon your friends and you distinguish them; you see the color of their hair and eyes, and you note their mode of apparel. But you do all this unconsciously, that is, with no conscious thought as to whether they are material, mental, or spiritual beings.

If you wish, you could gaze into the mirror at your side and see your own reflection—a body to be sure: hair, eyes, hands and feet, also apparel. You run down the stairs, but you do not give your feet a thought. You sit at a table and perhaps dine sumptuously, yet it does not occur to you that you have a stomach, and certainly you have not heard of indigestion. You dance upon the polished floor, and your joy and abandon are glorious. You are not considering whether or not your body is weary. You are not considering your body at all.

Should you feel impelled to sing to your friends, you give no thought as to whether or not your voice has been cultivated. It does not occur to you that you have a throat, yet laborlessly, wonderful tones now come forth, and words, too. But you quite take this for granted.

Now, you see that in your dreams you have hands and feet and body; you walk and run and sing and dance; you talk and play and eat. Although you are unconscious of a body, yet it accompanies you. Is this not so?

Turning now to this world, is it not easy to acknowledge that you perform many necessary and important acts relative to living, yet such action is quite unconscious on your part, and quite laborless, too? You waken in the morning, for instance, but you do not know how this is done.

You are quite unconcerned, however, as you have been doing this laborlessly for days, months, and years. It passes your attention unnoticed.

You partake of breakfast, yet you attend not to the digestion of this food or to the operations through which it passes in order to nourish the body. At night you go to sleep, but you have never yet discovered just how you do this little thing. Indeed, if you tried to investigate it, you might be unable to accomplish it.

When your body is radiant with the glow and glory of perfect health, you quite forget about it. The more health, the less thought of body; full health, no thought of body at all. Now, this by no means infers that we are bodiless, but it means that our body has no *personal* claim upon us. We should feel no responsibility regarding the body, and we should feel no attachment to it.

Has the hour struck for us when we are willing to be "absent from the body and present with the Lord"? Are we ready to yield attachment and responsibility that a personal sense of body brings? Are we not told in mystical language that it is in "losing" that one gains? Have no fear that in losing *attachment* to the body you may lose the body itself, for quite to the contrary, you will be fitting yourself to understand it.

Oh, wondrous, radiant light! Oh, glorious, ever-increasing revelation! To be willing not to heal or change the body is to find oneself on the royal road to a body that is not sick, limited, or changeable—a body immortal, eternal, and everlasting. *A body immune.*

It has been said that everything is as real as one makes it. Now, no one makes Reality, for Reality *is,* regardless of what anyone thinks or believes or feels. If one believes that his body is material—if a material body is reality to him—then automatically he subjects his body to so-called material action. But supposing one lays no claim to a separate, external, or personal body at all; would not he then be out of the touch of disease, limitation, destruction altogether?

Consider this momentous question slowly, meditatively. Finding the true idea of a thing, the false idea drops away automatically. Bearing this in mind, it would seem wisdom that we perceive why our bodies cannot be sick; then we will be fearless and immune. The time is here for each of us to see that we have no false body to deny, and that all form belongs to the one Life and Being.

Truth is not in any form, but Truth is every form. Being is not divided into form, but being is expressed by form. We cannot go out of Life, for we *are* Life. We cannot go out of health, for Life *is* health. We cannot be outside the kingdom, for the kingdom is *within* us. We cannot be separated from body, for body is one with Soul. We cannot be separated, divided, disunited. *We are complete and indivisible being.*

Since Reality is all, and all is Reality, then whatever the body is, it must be in and of Reality. Clear vision reports that Soul and body, Cause and effect, Life and form are *one*—now, always, and forever.

When we go to the telephone and listen to a friend's voice, we know that back of the instrument is the man himself, and the instrument is but the form or the medium of transmission. Now, it is quite the same with Soul and body, with Creator and creation. Form is the medium of expression. Form is as necessary and as eternal and indestructible as is the Self which it is expressing. Perfect embodiment is the body of Truth. Spirit blessed the form called *creation* and called this formation good, perfect, and ideal.

Do not worry about the teaching of reincarnation, which means the changing of forms; nor of pantheism, which means the placing of Spirit *in* creation. Soul is limitless, infinite, eternal—in everything and yet in nothing. Neither here nor there, yet everywhere. Neither this one nor that one, but everyone. The One shining in the star, sparkling in the water, blooming in the rose, ascending in the bird—seeing, hearing, feeling, expressing in all life and being.

Truth in the small, Truth in the great; Truth in heaven, Truth in earth. One Being, one All.

The One, all height and no height; the One, all time and no time; the One, all form and no form; the One, all language and no language; the One, all motion and no motion—the One indescribable, unspeakable, incomparable!

The One says: you are my infinite Self. All that *I* am, you are. All that is Mine is also thine. You are immortal being, including immortal form. Your form is My idea made visible. You are not something that has soul; you *are* Soul. Being is not something that has body; being *includes* body. As Soul is eternal, so also is body eternal. Body, form, is the expression of perfect, living Self-existence.

> Our Father Being, Hallowed be Our name.
> Our Kingdom is come; Our will is being done
> On earth as it is in heaven.
> We give this day of our daily bread;
> We joyously forgive all debts and debtors.
> We are not led into temptation,
> But we are delivered from all evil;
> For Thine, Mine, *Ours* is the kingdom,
> The power, and the glory forever.

Insight alone can sharpen the eye to function to fourth-dimensional vision and to right inter-pretation of a spiritual universe.

Fourth-dimensional sight is that sight which is able to see in the dark—"the light shineth in darkness"—which reports order instead of disorder, harmony instead of discord, unity instead of division.

Looking toward the self-existent heights, great seers have boldly proclaimed that evil has no existence whatever. Such vision swallows up duality as light takes up shadow.

Those of us visioning toward the city which "lieth foursquare" find it helpful to pore over in our minds words attuned to a higher order — words yielding nourishment to the mind like rain to the parched ground.

Let us inbreathe and breathe out such words as *infinity, eternity, freedom, victory, triumph, omniscience, omnipresence, omnipotence, almighty, everlasting, ascension.*

Let the cares and worries of false sense go, and vision the presence of Reality. Let the reports of mind and body go, and hear the voice of Christ.

Illusion is not in the thing itself. Illusion is in the false concept of that thing. Interpreting creation through the veils of time, space, and personality, is it any wonder that one reports division, duality, relativity?

Light is light, not darkness or twilight. A circle is a circle, not a square or a cube. Two and two are four, not three or five. And so perfect creation as pictured in the beginning (Genesis) and in the end (Revelation) is without spot or blemish—pure as crystal, scintillating as the most precious stone, radiantly reflective as the clearest mirror.

This brings to my remembrance a particular moment in which my mind swiftly and clearly functioned to ever-present reality despite the hearing of a false report.

I was wakened in the middle of a night's rest by the telephone. The report came that someone was suddenly ill, that an organ of the body was functioning very improperly. Coming out from a sound sleep, I said the first thing that came from my consciousness: "Tell him that two and two are four."

The person to whom I spoke thought that I was still sleeping or only partly awake, and refusing to accept my message, tried to induce me to send him a "spiritual" message, something that would be appropriate to his condition.

But I was adamant. That was what I saw, and that was my message. "Tell him that two and two are four!" That was final. That was all.

The following morning that man himself came to see me. He looked perfectly well, and he said he was perfectly well. "But what a queer message you sent me," he objected.

"Did you not find that you went immediately to sleep, that your 'attack' vanished?"

"Yes," he admitted. "That is true, but …"

"I will interpret that message for you," I said, "for the interpretation is the reality that healed you. I knew that you could not change Life or Its natural functions. The message that two and two are four means *Life is Life*. Life is not sickness, pain, and falsity. Life is perfect, changeless, glorious Being. Truth is that which *is*, and you can't change It. You are Reality, for there is nothing else for you to be."

This illustrates clearly that it is the *spontaneous* treatment which delivers—the treatment that leaps over words; that transcends dimensions; that standing alone declares a thing to be so because it is; that does not say: I will dress it in this gown or clothe it in these phrases so that it will be appropriate for the illusion; but boldly and with authority, Truth speaks from the heart, speaks from that blaze of glory which transcends dreams and dream language.

One should never hesitate to speak from his illumined state of consciousness at that precise moment, for then one is the Fire which consumes and the Power which delivers.

Life is not something that one may choose to believe, but life is what it is despite anyone's belief about it. Perfect, individual life, perfect functioning of that life, perfect glory and immortality of that life is independent of anyone's belief or thought about it. Let us therefore apprehend Life as It is, praise It as It is, express It as It is.

Perfect law of Spirit neither obeys nor disobeys mental and physical law. It is a law unto Itself. It is the Self-existent and Only. Its command is, "Let there be light! Let it come forth!"

Recognizing oneness in consciousness, the dove of peace again descends, and power is given to function to the Christ-Mind. But some may continue with material and mental methods of help and healing until they are ready for the higher position.

Our being is actually threefold—Father, Son, and Holy Ghost. In my textbook, *The One*, there is given a clear and scientific presentation of our Trinity-in-unity.

Should one read wonderful statements of Truth, absorbing these with eyes and ears only, not perceiving anything fresh or new about them but interpreting them through former belief and conviction, he receives no revelation of Truth, no inspiration or illumination.

But if as one reads, there comes forth a quick response from within him like the moving of a living thing—something warm, vital, uplifting like the blazing up of a living fire—this is revelation. One is then actively drinking of the River of the Water of Life.

Since our being is threefold, how do we interpret the Father, or first position, of our trinity? Since, "No man hath seen the Father at any time," the Father is the *unseen* presence. The Father of us is our unseen Life, Intelligence, Substance, and Reality. The Father is our irresistible Actuality, our changeless Being, our I AM.

Having meditated upon this first position and accepted it, one next takes up the Son. Who is the Son? Since the Father is the invisible Life, Truth, Being, Reality—who can the Son be?

The Son is Emmanuel, or God with us. The Son is therefore the Invisible *expressed*. The Son is Consciousness *individualized*—the individual being, the individual identity.

We are *both* the Father and the Son, both the Universal and the individual, and they are *one,* inseparable and indivisible.

We could not be the Father, Universal, without being also the Son, individual. The Father would be unidentified without the Son (individual identity), and the Son would have no being without the Father (Universal Substance).

The Holy Ghost is *Self*-illumination, *Self*-consciousness and Understanding *embodied.* To illustrate: we walk down the avenue and see a man carrying a sign, "I am blind." How can the Father, Son, and Holy Ghost be here? Well, the man is alive, and he would not be alive without Life. This unseen Life is God the Father.

He has individuality—he says "I"—and this individual identity is God the Son.

Now, why does he appear blind? Because of the veil of ignorance. He is not *consciously* aware of his spiritual identity. The fire in him has not been kindled. Although he is the sight of God, he acts like a blind man. But supposing that it came to him, or he heard, that he is a divine being; that his power to see is God, and thus he cannot be separated from his perfect sight.

Day by day it is with him. He sleeps with it; he eats with it; he continually feels, *I am a divine being; I am a perfect being; I am a God-being.* Finally this truth comes to absorb his mind completely. Then comes the blaze; then shines the glory. Illumination, inspiration leaps up within him and his sight is restored.

Now, this spiritual influx of light and glory which he has experienced is the Holy Ghost, and it is in this Light that he sees himself, that he finds his body manifesting his glory and his perfection. The coming of the Holy Ghost heralds the "healing."

The coming of the Holy Ghost is the *absorbing* of false beliefs, the *rising* into new joys, the *showing forth* of a body free from delusion.

"And Jesus said ... What I have done, all men will do; and what I am, all men will be."
— *The Aquarian Gospel*

"And his name shall be called the mighty God, the everlasting Father." —Isaiah

The notion that individual being is an image impedes individual spiritual advancement. Our individuality is the *one* Life, Truth, and Love. This Life, Truth, and Love was individualized, seen and interpreted as Jesus Christ; and this same Trinity-in-unity is individualized in you and in me. *Am I claiming it?* This each must answer for himself.

He advances most in understanding and demonstration who not only sees the heights, but aspires to the knowledge of Jesus Christ, individualizing infinite power and *demonstrating* the kingdom of heaven in his midst.

The perception that *we* are the Trinity, that individual being is Being individualized, delivers to us a fearless wing and mighty victory. Vision such as this, accompanied with fire of insight and courage of conviction, demonstrates the might of Omnipotence to the "pulling down of strong holds; casting down imaginations, and every high thing that exalteth itself against the knowledge of God" (2 Cor. 10:4-5).

Let us not be content with the letter of the Word, no matter how attractively we express it or how earnestly we listen to it. Let us aspire for *the spirit* of the Word! Of what avail are scientific words unaccompanied by "fire in the mouth"! Of what advantage is a fireplace stacked with logs when no match is provided?

Yea, the resplendent flame of Spirit in the twinkling of an eye consumes the false images of human thought, burns the chaff of erring belief, and lo, here stands individual spiritual being—the Christ—clothed in the mind of Omnipotence.

> "Behold, I will make my words in thy mouth fire." – Jer. 5:14

As we need both the match and the logs in order to obtain heat, so both the letter (understanding) and the Spirit (fire in the mouth) are demanded of us that we may put on our robe of glory and receive His name in our forehead.

Chapter III

THE SCIENCE OF OUR BEING

About half a century ago, a noted writer of metaphysical science stated in her textbook:

> That we are Spirit, and Spirit is God, is undeniably true ... The final understanding that we are Spirit must come ... At present we know not what we are; but this is certain, that we shall be Love, Life, and Truth, when we understand them.
>
> —Mary Baker Eddy

Has not the belief that we are human beings, subject to errors of the flesh, resulted in the limitation and discord enacted upon the face of the earth today? And will not the understanding that we are Soul, Spirit—the recognition and acceptance of the actuality of our being—be the truth that shall set us free from this false belief?

By identifying self as Life, Soul, one automatically rises to new heights.

"I, if I be lifted up, will draw all men unto me," spoke Jesus Christ. As peerless Christ-Truth is lifted before our vision, recognition and understanding take place, and our whole universe reflects this glory.

"Ye must be born again" was Jesus' testimony. The act of yielding up untrue beliefs for true understanding constitutes this rebirth.

Was it not because Jesus claimed and acted his *deity* that he infuriated the Jews? "This man," thought they, "who wears clothes, who eats and drinks and sleeps exactly the same as we do, claiming that he is God, claiming that he is different from us—we are human and he is human."

And so they said to Jesus, "For a good work we stone thee not; but for blasphemy; and because that thou, being a man, makest thyself God." (John 10:33).

They had insight enough to see that Jesus individualized almighty power in healing the sick and in raising the dead, but their ignorance and human sense kept them from perceiving that Jesus not only claimed this almighty authority for himself, but that he claimed it for *everyone*.

Jesus was the ideal Self. He was God in the flesh. And whatever is true of Jesus is likewise true of us all. No wonder we love to talk about Jesus. His great love for mankind prompted him to demonstrate to the very end his absolute understanding of unchangeable life and being—to portray to the whole universe that he had the keys to heaven.

> I love to tell the story
> Of unseen things above;
> Of Jesus and his glory,
> Of Jesus and his love.
> —Katherine Hankey

Can we perceive that we are Life, Truth, and Love except we first perceive that Jesus was Life, Truth, and Love? We cannot.

> "No man cometh unto the Father but by me. … Other foundation can no man lay than Jesus Christ … He that acknowledgeth the Son hath the Father also."

The study of the life of Jesus touches our hearts, wakens our love, and as we identify Self as Christ, we identify Self as Life, Truth, glory, and power.

Whatever Jesus claimed for himself, he claimed also for us. Hear his vibrant, startling words: "That they all may be one in us ... And the glory which thou gavest me, I have given them … that they may be made perfect in one."

The Christ (true belief) of you says: "*I* am the Life. *I* am the Truth. *I* am the Father. *I* am God." The human (untrue sense) says: "I am in limitation. I am in prison. I am in bondage."

Shall we identify ourselves as limited, human beings, or shall we identify ourselves as free, flawless, triumphant Christ? Let Absolute Science decide for us. Absolute Science is the science of high vision, ascending from glory to glory.

47

A great vision of Reality now sweeps over the world. Soon it will be more universally perceived and accepted that life is not a problem for the individual to solve. Its solution has already been reached. It remains now for the individual to *accept* the solution and *experience* the glory.

It is not that our health, for instance, is coming to us, but rather is it that our health is *here*. According to individual recognition of this fact does this health appear. It is not that the kingdom of heaven is coming to us, nor is it that earth is evolving into heaven, but the fact for our attention is that perfection is here—*reality is at hand.*

How much of heaven are we perceiving? As much as our individual state of consciousness permits.

"Agree with thine adversary quickly," directed Jesus. Reach a positive position of agreement and perception. "Nothing shall by any means hurt you," continued he who knew. We do not shoulder a gun and go forth into an external universe to attack our enemy, but right where we are we stand still and *behold* our salvation. We acknowledge it. We accept it.

We believe that because Spirit is all and is infinite, that we are this Infinity. How could it be otherwise? Since Reality cannot be separated or divided, *we* are this Reality. It is easy enough to believe that God-Self cannot lack; God-Self cannot be afraid; God-Self cannot be limited; God-Self cannot be destroyed.

It is said that the one of vision sees nothing but good, just as "to the pure all things are pure." The one of vision sees goodness not as the opposite of evil (un-good), but he sees goodness as *Omnipresence*.

The same with health. One of vision does not see health as the opposite of sickness, but he sees health as wholeness and as ever-presence. One of insight reports according to the vision of Reality.

Preach deliverance to those who are held captive by matter and mind (untrue belief)! As light kindles light, so recognition and praise of the Jesus Christ-Self brings forth radiance and glory of mind that *cannot* be deceived, of body that *cannot* be sick, of being which is verily Christ.

When thought is raised to the true state of being—the sense of Spirit—it is the mind of Christ.

Jesus brought to this world a way out of ignorance. He showed a path which was neither warfare nor separation, but on the contrary, was at-one-ment, oneness, and unity. Jesus' vision was to "agree." Yea—he himself was this at-one-ment or agreement.

Had Jesus come into this world clothed in the body of ascension, he would not have been seen here; but, "He took upon himself the form of a servant, and was made in the likeness of men," that he might be visible to those in this state of consciousness. From position of oneness with us he showed us his actual state of being—*our* actual and perfect state of being.

Jesus himself was our Way. He unified, he blessed, he forgave, he fulfilled, he agreed, and he redeemed.

Did Lazarus come forth as a living being because Jesus called him? No. It was because he *was* a living being that Jesus called him.

Was it because of lack of food that Jesus supplied baskets full of bread and fish? No. It was because of *abundance* of food that Jesus did this very thing.

Was it because the man's arm was withered and lifeless that Jesus told him to stretch it forth? No. It was because his arm was perfect and changeless that Jesus commanded: *stretch it forth!*

Was it because Jesus was functioning to opposites that he walked triumphantly upon the waves, passed invisible through the multitude, commanded the sick to be as the well, perceived the "sinning woman" as sinless and the so-called dead as the living?

It was because Jesus functioned in unity, in indivisibility, in oneness in his kingdom *here* and on earth *now* that he enacted this power.

Jesus' advice was to *leave the so-called external world alone.* "I walk in it," he said, "but I am not of it; I am not affected by it. I eat the food from the table, true, but I have other food as well. I live and eat and walk in your world, apparently, but to myself I am living and eating and walking in a world that you do not as yet comprehend. This world is the world I have told you about — the kingdom of Soul."

Jesus did not present any outer way of atonement, but he did show us an inner way — a spiritual recognition that is to take place within *individual* consciousness.

The following steps are to be taken by the individual as he rises from sense to Soul, individually ascending the ladder of life.

FIRST: Recognition that the so-called external universe is not external, but is picturization, or expression of thought and vision.

SECOND: Recognition that the belief in so-called evil indicates a lack of individual consciousness of the understanding of fullness, oneness, completeness, and unity.

TIIIRD: The final state is the immersion of individual sense into full, clear vision of Reality. The individual has now accomplished his at-one-ment and is resurrected into the "new man," the Christ-Self, the God-being who, ascending above all earthly beliefs, functions in Reality.

We read in Genesis: "And God saw everything that he had made, and, behold, it was very good." The perfect Creator and perfect Creation here mentioned portrays infinite Spirit and Its infinite manifestation as All-in-all. All life is pronounced immortal, changeless, eternal, and all manifestation perfect and good.

Now Genesis, in continuing, mentions a second creation appearing after the first. What can this second creation be except an untrue interpretation of the first? Or the first perfect and complete Creation seen materially instead of spiritually; seen imperfectly and incompletely instead of seen perfectly and completely; seen darkly as through a glass instead of seen clearly face-to-face?

A spiritual, individual being shall "know the truth" — shall know his power, his might, his dominion, his joy, his peace, his wonder, his eternity, his infinity, his wholeness, and his invariableness.

Therefore, we behold right here and now the actual truth of Creator and Creation. Moses speaks of the second creation as a (mental) "mist," and Paul calls it a "riddle," while St. John (of clearer vision) looked through the superimposition and testified to seeing the finished kingdom *here, at hand*. The discerning Jesus continually called attention to the perfect world as *now* in our midst.

Individual consciousness interprets the perfect Creation in degrees — "line upon line, precept upon precept, here a little, and there a little," and as vision enlarges, one beholds more and more completely the perfection which is prepared.

Take, for instance, the material ways of locomotion. Instead of being instantly where one wishes to be, as Jesus perfectly demonstrated, there came to this world at one time the vision of the stagecoach. Then, as clearer spiritual vision followed, this was interpreted or represented variously and successively by the steam engine, the electric engine, the automobile, and the airplane.

Today the airplane is man's exhibit of his highest concept of instantaneity. With a little more clearing of the mist, there will come even a fleeter and more easily constructed device, and later man will find something no larger than his own body which will carry him easily and swiftly over land and water. Finally, the greater Light will reveal that one can carry his own body triumphantly through space, directed only by his own thought and will.

Today, rigid progress is seen in all manner of inventions, discoveries, facilities of all kinds and natures, and this progress in material ways is taking place only because of the great advance in spiritual vision. Multitudes all over the world are applying their vision of Reality, of the perfect Creation, of the Jesus Christ presence to the transcendence of all false beliefs, and day by day we are reaching that vision which sees *face-to- face.*

This spiritual vision of oneself as free, flawless being blesses the mental plane, and mind begins to take on new thought and new ideas. Brotherhood is expressed as never before; a blending of hearts is being observed, not only with individuals, but with countries and with nations.

Spiritual vision blesses, too, the physical plane of action. Both mental and physical planes are controlled by spiritual understanding. People are eating, dressing differently, appearing differently everywhere—everything, everyone, constantly rising from glory to glory.

Said the prophet Isaiah:

> "Woe unto them that call evil good, and good evil; that put darkness for light, and light for darkness."

Since the world, as far as we are concerned, is our consciousness of it, *evil* and *good* are terms which mean to one his concept of them. One who knows in his heart the allness of good (because of the allness of God) undertakes not to expound to a brother, unenlightened by truth, the nothingness of evil, but he preaches to him repentance.

Repent of what? Those who believe that erring sense is reality and power must repent and forsake this false view, for not until one spiritually perceives the allness and ever-presence of good does he claim and comprehend the nothingness (in itself) of evil.

To call evil, good, and good, evil, is to be double-visioned—is to see both good and evil as power. As one worships and understands Reality, he discards untrue belief and refuses temptation. Spiritual healing is Spirit conscious of Its totality. Any superimposition, any erring condition that one seems to manifest can be dissipated by the living Truth, by Christ-Consciousness. Spiritual healing is evidence that all discord and limitation are unreal.

Jesus cast out false beliefs because of the Truth *in himself*. When it is stated that the world exists in us, that our world is our consciousness of it, it means that whatever we accept as reality, as power, as presence, constitutes our world at that time.

The following is an example. A woman on a busy street in the city suddenly noticed a great crowd of people collected, blocking traffic. Moving along until she saw the cause of the commotion, her eyes reported an accident. A horse and automobile had come together, and a man lay underneath.

Now, as this woman looked, this panorama of excitement, commotion, and accident was reported to her external world—her eyes—but she heard a voice very close at hand, the voice of her inner world, and it said, "Never mind what these people are seeing. What are you seeing?"

"Yes, what am I seeing?" she quickly asked herself. "Why—why, I am seeing heaven," she cried joyously, unconsciously moving away. "There are no accidents in my world. In my world there is eternal, changeless order and delight." The incident was wiped absolutely from her mind as happily she continued her way.

Several weeks later she happened to meet a friend who, not knowing she had been near the scene of the disaster, began relating it to her, stating that she had stood in the crowd and had seen the whole thing. "And the strangest thing of all happened," she went on. "Suddenly it all seemed to be over. The people seemed to be on their way without any departure; the horse became quiet; the trampled man stood up refusing assistance; and the havoc and excitement changed to order and normality like a miracle." But that other, the one who walked in her own world, she knew and understood, for in her world she had seen face-to-face.

It is inherent in each individual to know himself, to express himself, to *be* himself. As individual perception coalesces with true Consciousness, false belief slips from mind as a dream, and manifestation is seen in its true light. Thus, one sees creation according to his individual state of consciousness. One sees the so-called outer world according to his spiritual awakening.

In which world are we living? Are we living in a material world affected by every wind that blows—believing what eyes report, what ears hear, and what mind sanctions?

Or are we living in a perfect world, visioning with eyes of Spirit, listening with ears attuned to Truth, functioning with mind which is none other than the mind of Christ?

Truly our world is our consciousness of it. It is not a question with us how much wrong thinking, wrong living there is in it; rather is it a question with each of us: how much true belief have we accepted into our consciousness?

It has been truly said, "Without vision the people perish." Without vision of the spiritual, perfect universe, the kingdom within the Soul, the people perish—for, visioning outward things such as purport to be sickness, sin, death, is it any wonder that one should perish by reason of these very things which he visions?

Let us bring our light into our world and let it shine. Let us see no separation, destruction, or opposition, but only oneness, unity, omnipresence. So shall resurrection take place in you and in me; and as resurrection takes place in us, this glory from on high shall illumine our whole universe and all of our affairs.

We come not forth to battle with darkness, neither with thoughts or weapons. Light eliminates darkness laborlessly. We do not make a wall between light and darkness, but bring false beliefs right into the presence of our true Self. "I am the light," cried the invincible Jesus. This Light is within you, within me—the Light that will lighten any darkened sense—for Self is Light, and to be Self is to be Light.

Jesus continually turned his vision to the Light—his true perfect Being. This enabled him to transcend and transmute experiences of this world and led him to resurrection and ascension.

Jesus, in the apparent giving up of his sense of life, demonstrated *eternality of Consciousness.* God could not die—neither could Jesus. He could die to appearance, die to a double-visioned universe, but he could not die *to himself.*

Verily, this was the claim of Jesus: "I am the atonement! I am the resurrection! I am the ascension!"

We have entered a period of a tremendous awakening. Progress and revelation such as the world has never before known has appeared to human consciousness. This is the day of the emancipation of humanity. As centuries ago the southern slave found his slavery taken from him, so are human beings today having human limitations taken from them—limitations of time, age, disease, and discord.

These falsities of bondage and limitation are being outlawed through perception of one's spiritual, eternal, irresistible nature.

Great inspiration and illumination are coming rapidly over the whole world. This is the age of surprises, of visions, of unexpected discoveries. Day by day, hour by hour, heaven comes closer to the race consciousness. The signs of the times can now be read quite easily by one of insight.

Music, for instance, is rapidly assuming wider and wider proportions until soon music will be recognized as fourth-dimensional. No longer do we find music confined to four walls, but now we hear it in the streets, in the market places, in the automobiles, and even up over our heads in the sky. We can scarcely find a place where the burst of a song or a melody does not come upon our ears.

Often, too, it is reported that one hears tones other than those from the radio; he hears the music from the super-world. Such melody is undimensional, unlimited, unconfined. It is to be expected that in this era of insight, or era of spiritual light, many wonderful things unheard of heretofore shall come to pass. Great changes are noticed taking place in governments, racial beliefs, creeds, and rituals.

As we contact the true idea of a thing, the false idea drops away automatically. As we lift our vision to the Self-existent heights, we surely find the reality of health, joy, and glory irresistibly entering our lives and radiating through all our experience.

There is no limitation, no spot or blemish upon the face of the whole Creation. The limitation imposed by one's false belief is illusion only. Jesus reported no evil. He said that nothing shall by any means hurt us; he promised that one could handle serpents quite harmlessly; that should one swallow poison, he need not be at all affected by the world's belief of such a procedure.

Let us acknowledge Jesus' promises to be true today. Let us declare:

> I do believe in the word of the living Christ. I worship the One. I identify myself with Him who said that we all may be one; that the works that he did, we shall do also. I have almighty and implicit faith in the spirit of Truth, in the unity of Being, in the glory of Soul.

There is one Substance in this world which is fixed, permanent, sounding down through the ages. *My words* shall not pass away. Heaven and earth shall pass away, but *My Word* shall never lose Its power, never fail to fulfill.

To perceive unity, we function from a place above reason, above the relative mentality.

Truth is above comparison! Truth is incomparable. It is not how much greater truth is than something else, or how much greater one belief is than another belief. We do away with comparisons. We see that truth *is*. When we measure our vision by this standard, we find that our kingdom is here "on earth as it is in heaven."

Let us tell ourself continually that the universe is within us; that we see without according to what we are perceiving within. We see in the mirror what is standing before the mirror. How can we expect to vision the One without, if we are not entertaining the One within? How can we perceive unity in the universe if we have not unity in our consciousness?

Yea—is it not the Christ in you who is your hope of glory? How should we hope to see the Christ without, if we have not yet found the Christ within? How many of us have failed to recognize Christ at our door because we were not feeling Christ in our hearts?

Is not clear Insight Lord of the dark as well as of the day? Was not Jesus Lord of earth as well as Lord of heaven—"Lord of heaven and earth"? Lift the veil from your eyes and behold the *oneness* of life, the *unity* of being, and see no separation, division, or comparison.

Truth is totality! Truth is therefore the only substance that is ever present.

One need put forth no vision to see light where light is present; but who is seeing the Light which shineth in darkness?

It is easy enough to behold the Christ in the smiling countenance, the radiant Soul; but who is visioning the Christ in the darkened and unillumined mentality? It is simple to see health where health is visibly present; but who is seeing health where health is not visibly present?

It would have been easy for great multitudes to have accepted Jesus as the Christ had he been born in a palace, but how few accepted him who was born in a manger!

It is easy for one to be brave and strong in the midst of harmony and peace; but how many of us are brave and strong in the midst of mighty trials, temptations, and dangers?

Who comes forth from the fiery flames with no smell of smoke upon his clothing? Who feels the everlasting arms underneath while falling into an abyss of darkness? Who hears the angel's voice in the midst of his Soul's darkest moment? Who sees dry land in the midst of the Red Sea?

He who has vision! He who has faith! He who has trust! He who has love! He who is visioning face-to-face.

Chapter IV

PRACTICAL DEMONSTRATION

Men, great as poets, mystics, saints, and reformers, are men of renunciation. They have renounced personality. They are not swayed by opinions or moved by praise or censure. They look to the Light shining in their own souls.

The bird does not trust to the twig that sways beneath his light weight upon it. He trusts to his wings. We may have houses and lands, friends and families, but we place not our trust in these; we place not our happiness and our safety here. We remember: "All my trust on Thee [Understanding] is stayed."

Truth is the health of our body. Truth is the breath of our life. Truth is the sparkle of our eyes, the laughter of our lips, the strength of our hands. How close Truth is to us. Hark! Listen to the robin. It is the One singing His song. The One is the beauty of the flower, the charm of the evening, the breath of the morning, the pulse of all being. Yea—the One is All-in-all.

No matter how far one may have wandered in the dream, no matter how low one may have fallen in belief, a welcome is ready for him who cries, "I will arise and go to my Father." The wayward son in the parable left his home of joy and abundance and started off to search life for himself. Time and experience brought him nothing but husks, unrest, disappointment. Finally he remembered how happy he had been with his father—what a comfortable home he had had there, how carefree and joyous he had been. Ah—what a fool to have left! What ignorance to have chosen darkness rather than light, husks rather than real substance. He would return.

But wait—how would he be received? Notwithstanding this doubt, he would go at once. And he returned just as he was—poor, weak, weary, heartsick, miserable in both mind and body.

And lo, he found everything the same as before he left. The moving of the hands of the clock had not changed a thing. All was the same as if he had never wandered away at all. Now he accepts the genuine substance; he lives the life his father desires, and he finds peace, joy, and glory. He has now "put on" that which was *already* for his acceptance!

It is like this with us. We oftimes forget our first awakening, our first blaze of glory, and our spontaneous gladness which, like a sparkling spring, bubbles from the living well within. Let us not abandon that vision of oneness enabling us to walk over waves and through Red Seas.

Is it not in recognizing the finished kingdom at hand, in accepting the Christ within, in speaking the Truth in His name, and in practicing the presence of the One that we grow more and more familiar with the Science of Ascension?

Remember, it is the heart and not the head that makes such things possible. The question for us all to consider and answer is: *am I practicing the presence of the One?*

Does not the One ask, "Can you hear My voice if you are looking to personality for guidance and uplift?" Books and teachers of Truth deliver a light which enables one in a wonderful way to see this Truth in his own heart. They help one to place his radical reliance upon Christ as the almighty Power, the changeless and imperishable Reality.

We bring the sense of a separate or personal state to the impersonal or God-state, and we begin a new life. Laying down the untrue for the true, the limited for the actual, the temporal for the eternal, we find "the peace of God, which passeth [human] understanding."

We hear the Voice: "I came to earth as Jesus Christ to show you how to transcend the human state, the earth-state, and how to perceive and accept your perfect God-being."

"But why is this dream-state necessary?" you ask. "Why am I seeing that which is called time, space, personality, sin, sickness, and discord?"

"If Intelligence did not manifest as such, what were the use then of Intelligence? If power were inert, dormant, unexpressed, of what avail then were that power? If love were unknown, unfelt, untold, of what delight were such love? Can you not recall that when you have been lifted on high—when you have received great illumination, when sickness has rolled back like dew before the sun, when sorrow has subsided like darkness before the light—that this has been the moment when you were transfused with rapturous joy, with unutterable peace, power, and glory? Then you have *known* Truth. Then you have *felt* Love. Then you have *manifested* even that which you are—Myself."

Now, it may seem to the unenlightened consciousness that one is a human being born of human parents and that through experience one progresses to health, joy, and peace. However, the announcement of Truth, the gospel of Jesus, proclaims that inherently we are divine beings now; that the road called progress and experience does not create our perfection, but rather does it disclose and reveal our perfection.

Today on every hand we find people searching for health. This is similar to one searching for the glasses which rest upon his nose; like one dying of hunger while gold fills his purse. Searching, traveling, and seeking *externally* takes one in a wrong direction. He seeks that which he already is. The River of the Water of Life abides in him and is his everlasting health.

Jesus left a message: Behold, the kingdom of everlasting life is here, at hand. Look thou upon the fields *already* white to harvest!

Therefore, we find that the true way, or the illumined path, is not something to be attained externally, but rather is it something to be inwardly revealed. Christ stands in our midst saying, "Peace, be still!" His message is: in you is the water of Life. In you is the heavenly kingdom.

"Cast your care upon Me," says the inner Voice. The radiance and quickening inspiration is of the Holy Ghost, instantly forgiving sins or mistakes and instantly placing the body under heavenly law. Miracles attend the coming of our Christ. Never doubt but that your hour of fulfillment is at hand. Lifting our vision to spiritual Reality, we find this Reality entering our being and all of our affairs. Our minds, renewed and refreshed, are filled with joyous praise and glory. We find it a very easy thing now to be absent from the body and present with our Lord-Self.

A falsity, of course, has no substance back of it, nothing to hold or sustain it, and its fabulous existence is bound to be discovered. The redemption

67

of mental darkness consists in accepting the light of Truth.

There is told a story of some savages who lived in a dark cave in a certain part of the Himalayas. They had never seen the light of a fire. These savages cooked their food as best they could by the heat of the sun. They went to bed and arose the day following by solar light. As time went on they began to wish that they might see what was in the depths of this great cave in which they lived. Day by day they longed to drive out this terrible darkness, and they believed that evil spirits and great monsters were moving around here; in fact, they imagined that they saw them.

Someone told them that this terrible monster—darkness—would leave if they would worship it. They followed this suggestion faithfully. They beseeched and supplicated the darkness, but it remained as unyielding as before. Then they were told to fight this dark being—to take clubs and strike and beat it into submission. However, with their clubs and weapons they did but strike one another, and this device was soon abandoned as unfeasible. They also tried fasting and other practices, but all to no end. The darkness was as great as ever.

Finally a man came along who told them that the only thing that could make darkness leave was a light. This man asked for some straw and bamboo sticks, and by striking a stone against a piece of flint there came a spark. Soon, by means of the twigs and straws, the long bamboo stick began to blaze. The savages now followed this man as he entered the great black cave, and lo, the darkness was not there!

They thoroughly searched the cave but could find no evil spirits, no monsters; nor could they find the darkness, for wherever they carried the light, behold, there was only light. At last their wish was granted. The darkness left.

Now, after one has perceived the true Light, and after this Light has taken away some of his darkness, he can never again believe so completely in that darkness as reality. It is this way after one has glimpsed the finished kingdom. Never again is a world of time, space, and personality quite so real to him. As one passes above the plane of thought and looks up and out into the perfect land, he automatically becomes filled with new ecstasy and new joy that never before has been equaled in his experience.

This land of prepared glory which he now beholds is one in which there is no separation of people, things, or ideas whatsoever. Here one is unbounded, unlimited, free as air. Here beautiful thoughts come bubbling from one like sparkling elixir. One sees a universe of truth and love, of joyous splendor and ever-increasing glory. No suggestion of sin, of fear, of sickness, or destruction is thought here, for this is the realm of perfect light; this is the realm of ideal harmony; this is the heavenly kingdom; this is the place of the heart.

Now, after one has experienced such inspiration—the lighting of the fire within the self, the removal of the darkness—he finds that spiritual affirmations become more and more alive to him. No longer do sentences mean mere words to him like so many letters of the alphabet joined together, but now they take on fresh meaning. Something even seems shining upon the pages of the book which he is reading, and the words are like living things. One feels a great expansion—a freedom and an independence not known before.

After one has caught glimpses of the finished kingdom, a new language is his—a new tongue. Many words now reveal new meaning to him; for instance, the word *health*. One used to think of health as identified with the body, but now he sees that health is universal and is on the mountaintop or in the dungeon. Health is unlimited and omnipresent, like the sunshine and like the fact that two and two are four. Health is a fact of being. Health is indivisible Omnipresence.

The word *health* is placed with great words such as *infinity, eternity, freedom, life, love, peace, and power*. We vision a perfect universe. We behold a living Christ. We believe that good and abundance, health and harmony are of a universal Substance.

Not by strength of body nor by might of mind, but *by My Spirit,* saith our Lord-Self. Now, the Spirit of the Lord in one is perfect, ideal being. The Spirit of the Lord is that health which is in everything, but attached to nothing, for health is Reality.

Spirit is the fact that, "The desert shall rejoice, and blossom as the rose ... the eyes of the blind shall be opened, and the ears of the deaf shall be unstopped ... the lame man shall leap ... and the tongue of the dumb shall sing." Spirit is the fact that there is no limit of health to the body, no limit of understanding to the mind. There is no division, no limitation, no attachment in being.

Spirit is the fact that there is no stopping place for life, no boundary to health, no termination for joy, peace, or delight. Spirit is the fact that we are living *now* and that this life will never cease for one instant to be; that we are a being of intelligence, power, glory without end; that we are divine, eternal, irresistible Soul, Self, Truth.

We drink the water of Life freely, and the path of illumination shines bright with living glory. The presence of the One is seen, known, felt, and understood. The Golden Age is here—the age of boundless freedom, of indescribable splendor, love, and glory.

71

God-being is not subject to material law any more than a bird is subject to the laws governing vegetables. We recognize, affirm, and declare that we as God-being are not subject to the laws of matter, but that we are *free in heavenly Reality*. With burning zeal and with fire of insight, we insist that we are immune from all sense of evil, bondage, and limitation. Jesus declared that none of these things (material beliefs) could harm us, for there is no harm in unreality.

The conditions pictured in the body and called disease are not at all as they seem to unenlightened vision. The report of the senses is that the disease is in or on the body; that the trouble is *external*. This is altogether an erroneous idea, for what is seen in the body and termed disease is *picture* only and is no more in the body than a horse pictured on the motion picture screen is on the screen. The perception of this one point alone brings great relief and freedom.

As we correct untrue thoughts (darkness) with right spiritual ideas (light), simultaneously the picturization changes, and instead of disease (darkness) there is now health (light).

Let us acquaint ourself with true spiritual ideas. One of the first to establish as a working basis is that *we are Spirit, God*. This fact accepted, it is then easy to perceive that spiritual being is not subject to false beliefs. A God-being cannot believe falsely, but is forever conscious of harmony and changeless reality.

No false picture exists in the mind of Christ, and our heritage is this mind. What harm can a false thing do? We perceive that Truth is with us and so nothing can be against us. We realize that a false idea is no idea at all; we cease fearing it.

Filling our consciousness with divine ideas— ideas of reality, of love, of peace, of omnipotence, of victory—we ask, "What is there that can hinder us from expressing that marvelous being which we are? What is there to keep us from that wonderful glory which is ready and prepared for us? Can anything oppose Almighty Truth? Can anything prevent our response when Almighty Truth claims us?

We insist that, being Soul, we cannot lose our vision of eternal, changeless, and harmonious existence. Our vision is clear and constant. Our ideas are pure and complete. Our bodies are one with true Consciousness, hence they are free from all falsity and from all imperfection whatsoever.

Pictures can move rapidly on the picture screen, yet nothing is actually taking place on the screen; nothing is being healed or removed or changed. Attention is given to the machine (mind), and the picture (expression) follows automatically.

Perceiving that there is no kingdom of darkness, that the kingdom within us is the kingdom of everlasting Light, we arise new-born. We shout our freedom from limitation. We hold fast to reality and we say, "What can separate us from the all-Power? What can overthrow the omnipotence of our divinity?"

Thus, correcting material beliefs with spiritual ideas, we commence to experience a new world. We have not created our health and harmony, but we have taken possession of them. We have awakened to the fact of the perfect health and harmony *at hand.*

Surely there is a Power irresistible, able to do all things. Let those of us who are seeing and feeling this Light bring It to other hearts longing and waiting for Its arrival. The presence of the living Truth is sweeping this universe, making Itself known, seen, felt; hour by hour ushering in the Golden Age wherein are boundless freedom, indescribable splendor, irresistible love, and transcendent glory.

You are not divided into a soul, a mind, and a body. The body is the means through which Soul, Being, brings Itself into expression, action. Body is as imperishable, undeniable, indestructible, everlasting, eternal as Being—for *Being and body are one.* We are Being, action, form. We cannot be separated, divided, disunited. Creator, creating, and creation comprise one unit.

Let all sense of division and separateness depart from thought. We are not trying to unite God and man, Soul and body, for clear vision reports that God and man, Soul and body, Cause and effect, Life and form, are one *now, always, and forever.*

Every hour earth is taking on more of the glory of heaven, and from glory to glory we press forward. Deserts are becoming fertile; valleys are blossoming forth. Cities, countries, nations are daily uniting in thought, and the result will be peace and power. We are facing the seventh angel—the day of fulfillment and rest.

Let us acknowledge that the time is come, the hour is here. The angel of insight gently whispers, "Be of good cheer" over all the earth. The Bible instructs us that the body is transformed by the renewing baptism of Spirit; therefore, being new-born in Spirit and putting on (accepting) our inherent immortality, we gently and laborlessly transcend inharmonious experience. Mind imbued with spiritual understanding is a law unto Itself—dispelling illusions and blotting out erring beliefs.

When Spirit is seen and accepted to be the life of all—when it is certain to us that we all have the same life, the same being, the same reality—then the divine body will appear.

Progress is a term applied to human existence wherein the sense called mortal, through states and stages of consciousness, progresses to the point of ascension—the final triumph over all beliefs of mortal being and mortal universe.

Spirit is not regenerated. It is humanity that is regenerated. How can we understand God except through spiritualization of thought? Dematerialization and spiritualization is one process. In this process of vision and practical demonstration, sense (mortality) seems to pass through three distinct stages before yielding completely to Truth (immortality). These three stages are called the atonement, the resurrection, and the ascension.

Atonement is the dawning upon human consciousness of one's sinless, perfect state. Atonement is perception that as "light shineth in darkness," it is therefore impossible for evil to be evil. One perceives that inasmuch as the universe is primarily in one's consciousness, there is therefore no *external* evil. What is called evil is like the cloud that would conceal the light. The light shines, constantly and uninterruptedly.

Always the good is shining in consciousness, but when mists of sense obscure the good, then the result has been termed "evil." Atonement, therefore, is perception of *one* Presence as *always* present. It is perception that all that changes is belief. That which has been called evil, such as disease, destruction, and death, are the results of false sense—results of not clearly perceiving the Light which is always shining.

Atonement perceives that correction is to take place inwardly. The outward follows automatically. That which needs correction is mistaken sense. One perceives that untrue (false) beliefs are to be corrected by the acceptance in our consciousness of genuinely true ideas.

Resurrection, the second step leading from sense to Soul, is the *practice* of atonement. Resurrection is practical demonstration. Resurrection is restoration—the restoring to the mind of power, might, glory, and dominion; the restoring of that which was never lost or lacking except in belief. Resurrection is the *practice* of right vision and the *practice* of right ideas.

Resurrection is self-improvement in sense and thought. As higher and higher concepts of health and immortality are delivered, naturally one embodies and expresses them. It is this living process of resurrection that has been called "practicing the Presence."

Resurrection is the period delivering abatement of so-called evil. It is self-purification. It is awakening from the dream of opposites to the perception and acceptance of oneness.

Ascension is one's utter renunciation of all that constitutes mortality, and it is the attainment in consciousness of one's eternal individual identity.

Ascension is the return, in belief, of the prodigal to his father's home—his real state of being. Having taken the footsteps of atonement (right perception of reality and unreality) and having taken the step following called resurrection (practice of the One as All), the prodigal (mortal) has entirely lost his sense of mortality and has gained the sense of spiritual pre-existence. He now enters his spiritual rest and finds eternal peace.

As we learn the way in Absolute Science and enlarge our spiritual capacity for a higher life, we individualize sovereign power and demonstrate the falsity of bondage and limitation.

The Science of Ascension, revealed to the waiting heart, opens prison doors to those who are bound and sets the captive free.

Spiritual ideas, delivering to us a spiritual sense, lead us to divine heights and make it possible for us to exchange a material sense of existence for Soul-existence. As consciousness is uplifted, one gently relinquishes untrue beliefs and notions, demonstrating his divine authority in overcoming sin, sickness, and discord.

Exercising his inherent authority, one rises to the enraptured perception of Self as dwelling in infinite harmony—complete, perfect, immutable, and incorruptible.

As material sense (the sense reporting pain, limitation, and discord) is perceived as false, and as spiritual sense (the sense of health, joy, and harmony) is recognized as the *real* sense, one begins to utilize his infinite power to establish in his daily experience a perfectly harmonious existence.

We are delivered to Truth as we accept and embody Truth. This is not a method of mind over matter, nor is it mind over mind, but it is the divine process of spiritualizing thought and sense, demonstrating the omnipotence of Truth over false beliefs and enforcing the spiritual act of Soul over false sense. Truth is victorious, supreme, and gloriously omnipotent. The consciousness of this fact redeems sense from fear, renews faith, and exalts the affections.

Gaining the vision of Self as eternal Life, irresistible Truth, and exalting Love, we lose fear and boldly enforce our understanding.

Beholding the truth of our being and accepting our heritage—our reality as the Christ-Self—we unhesitatingly stand firm in our faith, knowing that the Holy Ghost dwells with us.

What is the ultimate of so-called attainment but ascension? Is this not the victory that is prepared for us—the overcoming of all belief in sin, sickness, limitation and the crowning triumph over death? Not a thing but false sense conceals Reality from us, and not a thing but spiritualization of thought and vision opens to us the gates of paradise revealing ascension above earthly sense.

What can melt away the sense of fear and darkness except the understanding of true being? Understanding is the Light which places the feet on firm ground, establishing Its principle by demonstration.

The kingdom of all-inclusive good never disappeared from spiritual sight but remains forever intact, omnipresent, and tangible to immortal Consciousness.

The kingdom of eternal, uninterrupted harmony awaits individual recognition and acceptance. In proportion as human consciousness becomes divine is the perfection and completeness of Self realized and embodied. Clad with divine illumination and spiritual perception, we assert our mastery over disease, fear, and bondage, and we prove irrefutably that divine understanding is supreme and triumphant. Waking to the perception of Self as God-being, we are lifted to a higher plane of experience and find it possible to demonstrate health and harmony.

The awakened consciousness sees but one way—the Self. "I am the way." Truth leads the eager and ready heart onward and upward, advancing it spiritually and disclosing the ultimate perception that the kingdom of everlasting harmony and glory is within one's own power and demonstration.

Practical demonstration is the act of Truth destroying material beliefs and uplifting faith and vision to discern perfect Creation—permanent, changeless, untouched by any dream sense. As Reality is brought to light, human sense is resurrected, and the spiritual idea of life is revealed as ever-operative and practical.

Those instructed in Absolute Science have grasped the glorious view of Self as all-knowing, all-mighty, and all-inclusive; and practicing this inspiring view, they ascend the scale of being and emerge gently into Life everlasting.

Let us know and demonstrate that an improved belief cannot retrograde. Once we gain control of erring sense through Soul or spiritual understanding, let us stand firm and unfaltering, realizing that nothing can deprive us of our complete demonstration of health, harmony, and happiness.

All there is to sickness, sin, and death is a false claim—a claim of falsity which cannot dethrone Soul or deprive anyone of his continuous sense of life and immortality. There is but one right vision—the fact of perfect Being, perfect ideas, and perfect expression. Holding thought to this ideal, we master so-called material law and annul its erring sentence. This divine practice in its direct application to human needs lifts individual consciousness above physical sense, removes fear and false belief, and reveals the all-power and ever-presence of our kingship and kingdom.

Absolute Science, lifting one's consciousness higher in the scale of being, reveals to him that identifying himself as Christ, he is free, victorious, and triumphant.

This spiritual understanding discloses individual might and power and reveals the phenomenon of Ascension.

Chapter V

RIGHT INTERPRETATION

It is stated that one can easily penetrate and expose untruth when he perceives the genuine and real, when he perceives the truth itself.

As soon as an untruth comes to one's attention, intuitively he feels the impulse to investigate the truth of the situation, for he knows that if he can discover the truth, the untruth will automatically be exposed and annulled.

Should someone bring information that does not seem true to us and we wish to ascertain if his report is actually true, we begin to trace his statement back to its origin or starting place, do we not? We unravel the story little by little until we are satisfied that we have arrived at the truth.

Looking through a veil, truth appears inverted, impossible; but stripping off the veil, we penetrate the mist and perceive the real to be real and the unreal to be nothing.

Now, it is easily understood that when a true statement is voiced or a true experience is placed before us, we do not investigate this, for there is no need of investigating harmony, peace, and contentment. But when something disturbing or disconcerting comes to our attention, the first impulse is to look up the truth and find out the actual facts.

We do not attend to the report itself, nor do we attend to the false situation or condition, but exercising spiritual vision, we look *beyond* the so-called material and erring testimony and perceive the truth that is standing back of it—the truth which seems concealed from view.

> "The light shineth in darkness, and the darkness comprehendeth it not."—John

If we perceive the Light that is shining, we simultaneously expose the darkness which is comprehending It not. Looking toward this Light and meditating, it comes to us that a condition of sleep and lapse from the actual state of being, or a condition of false and untrue belief, does not accord with the words of Jesus, "Ye are the light ... the kingdom is within you." We also recognize that back of the put-to-sleep belief there is a genuine fact of *perfect, changeless being,* and back of the untrue expression of inharmony and discord there shines the fact of *perfect, changeless, and immortal embodiment.*

We let not a sense of sympathy go toward the individual who claims to be experiencing falsely nor to the condition which he states is substantiating his mental claim. What is the onlooker seeing? Is he seeing the true universe truly? If so, there is no occasion for sympathy, fear, or disturbance. Is he beholding form corresponding to the spiritual vision of changeless, perfect, and immaculate being? If so, he is mindful of reality.

The *identity* which the onlooker reports, first as a crawling caterpillar and later as a beautiful butterfly, never changes, for individual identity is Self and is therefore constant, unchangeable, and immortal, no matter what any onlooker may be claiming.

This fact perceived, one grasps it so exultantly that he begins at once to interpret the universe according to reality.

Recognizing and accepting individual identity as forever established, perfect, and complete, without beginning and without end, he now perceives that any untrue expression presenting itself to physical vision and testifying to discord, disease, and disturbance is at variance with the premise and the principle of this changeless identity, and therefore cannot be accepted as carrying a vestige of truth.

No matter what may be the testimony of material sense, no matter what may be the testimony of darkness comprehending not the Light, the fact is that perfect being and perfect universe are *now at hand* for us to behold and experience.

Let it be clearly perceived that a being who at one time is called a mortal and at another time is called an immortal is one entity. A mortal is not an immortal, but this relative statement is understood as one correctly interprets it. It can be said that a caterpillar is not a butterfly, yet the onlooker knows that though he calls one form by a certain term and at another time by another term, he is all the time referring to the same entity.

Thus with individual being. With a clouded view, being is interpreted as mortal and human, while with spiritual vision, being is interpreted as perfect and divine. *The individual identity, however, is uninterrupted, constant, and eternal.*

When one is believing in something that is untrue, believing some false condition present which actually is not here, this state of mind is called in metaphysics "false belief." It is this false belief that one has to meet and overcome, and he meets and overcomes it with the right, with the Truth, with right interpretation.

Relatively speaking, that which causes darkness to disappear from a room is the light, and relatively, that which causes false or untrue belief to disappear from the mind is true belief. Belief in Truth is true belief and right interpretation, and as one exercises this right interpretation he finds the kingdom of heaven within his own consciousness.

A true belief has actual substance back of it. If one traces back the true belief, he arrives at the absolute Truth Itself. And if one traces back the untrue belief, he sees that as untruth it has no support whatsoever; it rests upon nothing, for it is but an untrue interpretation of that which is perfect and true.

This is why one need not sympathize with another who is apparently shadowing forth an untrue state. Instead of sympathizing with a mistake, a misrepresentation, one brings the light of Truth to that consciousness. One understands that in accepting true belief, he has Christ with him; he has Reality with him, and his victory is assured.

Therefore, one does not treat disease, sorrow, or any disorder as though it were actual, but he sees that this is the picturing forth of wrong belief in the mind, and that as soon as true belief is accepted, this Truth is the Light which spontaneously illumines his universe.

Holding to the perception that we are Life, we are Truth, we are Spirit, one feels firm ground under his feet, feels omnipotent Reality within him. With eyes clear and with feet firmly planted on that which *is*, the untrue expression vanishes and utterly disappears.

One is not misled, however, into thinking that any actual change has taken place, for such belief is not clear perception. It is simply that now one has a fuller consciousness of Reality, and he is expressing this improved belief.

"Nothing shall by any means hurt you," testified Jesus. It is as we perceive this tremendous fact of Reality and practice it in our vision, thinking, and acting that we ascend above untrue states and beliefs.

The vision of Ascension sees clearly that nothing external is to be healed, changed, or removed. We do not go out with vision, thought, or action to conquer discord. We go *within* always—and within we find Truth. And finding Truth, we rest in the consciousness that our being is Omniscience, Omnipotence and Omnipresence. This right interpretation uplifts human understanding—and Christ appears.

The putting on of immortality is not like the putting of a cloak upon one's shoulders or like the placing of gold into one's purse, but putting on immortality is like the receiving of something that one did not know that he already possesses. Children, for instance, put on "two and two are four." It appears as though they receive it outwardly or that they add it to their knowledge, whereas the fact is that the consciousness of this fact *already exists in them*.

It is written in a well-known metaphysical textbook: "Mortals will someday assert their freedom in the name of Almighty God." Mortals (those unillumined as to their actual perfection) are destined (because of their nature) to trace back their identity and to discover that this identity is the actual Truth.

Isaiah, looking into Reality, perceived that Jesus was the "Mighty God, the everlasting Father," and Jesus, visioning the kingdom of perfect Being, exclaimed, "that we all may be one."

In the story of the sheep and the lion cub, the latter lived for years as a sheep, not realizing his lion nature until a real lion presented itself before his vision. Likewise, people for many centuries considered themselves mortal and human until Reality came before their vision, and they recognized *themselves* as Reality.

In the story, the sheep-lion did not experience his real nature until he saw the majestic lion standing upon the hillside, outlined against the horizon. Gazing enraptured at this ideal, all of a sudden he felt something give way within him— his sheep belief vanished. Recognizing himself as lion, spontaneously he accepted his real nature and entered into his kingdom of the jungle and forest.

What a great lesson lies concealed in this simple parable. Covering the face of this earth were people who, believing they were human beings, experienced sickness, sin, and death in accordance with their false beliefs. But one day, looking up, lo! there standing before them was the glorious presence—"the Lion of the tribe of Judah"—a being of transcending glory and majesty.

Gazing rapturously at this Ideal, many felt something give way within them—their human beliefs vanished. Recognizing their God-being, spontaneously they accepted their real nature. and they entered their rightful heritage—the kingdom of perfection.

This Ideal Presence is here *today*, standing before all, for to those who look for Him doth He appear before them! "Lo, I am with you always. I will never leave thee nor forsake thee."

Beloved, we are looking upon this Christ—our ideal Self! We, too, have *felt* that false something give way in us, delivering us from the belief that we are human beings! We rapturously and spontaneously accept our kingship and our kingdom!

We see deliverance before us. We behold our kingdom at hand. We accept our Ideal standing on the mountain peak, outlined against the glowing horizon of victory, triumph, and ascension. Here stands our Identity—our Christ—with face like the sun and with raiment "as no fuller on earth could white them."

All hail! Behold our Identity. Behold our God-being!

We enter the paradise which is prepared for us in the beginning (Genesis) and which is prepared for us in the ending (Revelation), and entering, we find the peace which passeth verbal expression.

Now, in applying this sublime vision to the seeming problems of everyday experience, one finds that it brings him instant freedom, joy, and satisfaction to apprehend and realize the right interpretation of *time, place, and personality*.

For instance, time. One often feels that he is hindered by a sense of time. He feels that next week or next year more good will be disclosed to him than now, today. Abundance of good may seem to him to be in the future rather than right at hand.

What is the vision of our God-Self? Does this Self establish a difference between last year and today? Between today and a year from today? Verily, no. To the spiritual eye there is no division, no separation whatsoever. Whatever is true is always true. If it is ever true that I have abundance of all good, then this fact is true *now* and for *all* time.

The notion of separation from good is altogether false, and it can be proven very easily. Recently a telephone message came to me from a student asking for help. She stated that she did not know which way to turn for supply, that always her demonstration seemed depending upon some future arrangement which never came to pass and upon certain individuals who did not fulfill her expectations. Moving away from the telephone, the first thought that came to me was this:

> "One day is with the Lord as a thousand years, and a thousand years as one day."
>
> —Peter

It was radiantly clear to me that if the student would be helped next week or next year, she had received this help a thousand years ago. Eternity is here and at hand, "the same yesterday, today, and forever," and what is called a division of time, such as a day, a month, and a year, is merely material interpretation of changeless Reality.

In the material sense-kingdom we have time, but in the kingdom above the material sense, we have eternity. I considered this joyously, basking in the consciousness of never-beginning, never-ending eternity; and also I knew that as being is *one*, the student who asked for help was also conscious of this same Reality.

Recalling that she mentioned dependence in a business way upon those at a distance from her, I saw that distance, like time, is a false sense of belief in separation and division, and this false sense had no reality at all. Infinity cannot be divided or separated. It is *one* Presence. Whatever is "there" is also "here," for there and here are the same position—always (eternity), everywhere (infinity), unlimited abundance.

Then I accepted the nothingness of personality and realized that one's demonstration does not depend upon anyone but himself. Always, everywhere—*one being.*

About an hour later the same student called me again. She said that a wonderful experience had just come to her. A voice had spoken to her the name of a man whom she had not seen for over twenty years. I told her to go to him. Her next report was the practical demonstration. Through the help of this man, she was able to accomplish an extraordinary and gratifying sale which for over ten years she had struggled and failed to make.

Within, one finds the jewel. One is *himself* the way. Do you recall the parable of the king and the jewel? It seems that a certain king one day came upon a stone sparkling brilliantly in the clear waters of a lake. There before his eyes sparkled this beautiful gem. The lake was drained at the king's command, but the stone could not be found.

As soon as the water came into the lake, there appeared again the sparkling of the gem. Who could fathom this mystery? A sage was called in to counsel, and he immediately practiced right interpretation.

Calling a servant to him, the sage commanded that he climb a tall tree growing by the side of the lake. In its overhanging branches was found a crow's nest, and here among the sticks at the bottom of the nest rested the sparkling gem. What was seen in the water was not the actual gem itself, but only the reflection.

In the dream of material existence, one feels that he must seek hither and yonder. He must wait for the years to roll by. He must meet certain friends or individuals who are to help him on his way toward prosperity and happiness. But he is looking in the wrong direction; he is not practicing right interpretation, for he is looking out instead of in. The jewel is not in the outer expression. The jewel is *within*. The priceless, sparkling jewel is the Soul; is the Self. Looking within, one sees that always, everywhere, there is but *one Being*.

Seeing and feeling this confidently, calmly, soon the reflection appears in the universe (lake or mirror) before us. But we're not deceived. We see the sparkle; we rejoice in the demonstration, but we know that the jewel is within. We know that expression and realization are one and inseparable.

How can we experience transcending harmony and practical demonstration except by the right interpretation of Ascension? How can we exercise divine authority except by the illumination of spiritual sense?

This exalted spiritual sense is exercised through the inspiration of the heart. The spiritual power of glorified thought and vision, with no mental argument whatsoever, redeems one from false sense of imperfection.

There is a way above the path of trial and suffering. Reaching a higher sense through insight and revelation, one is able to demonstrate the Christ and rise *spontaneously*, easily, to the spiritual consciousness of being.

Jesus restored to human consciousness the lost sense of perfection, and he established this harmony, wholeness, joy, and happiness as the reality of our individual being. This divine process of right interpretation, acknowledged and accepted by the individual, enables him to subdue the material belief in sin, sickness, and limitation and to embody the triumph of Spirit.

We can see clearly enough that there is no actual transition from belief to understanding, but that transition, resurrection, and ascension seem essential to relative experience only.

We do not deny untrue beliefs or untrue expressions with the thought of destruction. On the contrary, we use denial with the spiritual insight and conviction that no destruction is necessary. "The law (of destruction} is not made for a righteous man" (1 Tim: 1:9).

In our night dreams we apparently move from one place to another place; we apparently change from one idea to another idea. But waking, we see that nothing whatever has taken place and that mental action or dream action is the same as nothing happening at all.

Preserving this perception, we understand that when we put off wrong beliefs and accept true understanding—when we put off mortality and put on immortality—this is only happening in a mental experience, for real being is eternally unchangeable.

True experience is changeless, irresistible Omnipresence. In the dream-experience, deliverance and emancipation from erring beliefs and erring conditions symbolize this freedom. Perfect individual identity is here, and as we waken to the perception and acceptance of this glorious fact, we behold this being in earth as in heaven.

Full consciousness of changeless being and of supernal Life brings deliverance from the dream-experience called sin, sickness, and death in the same way as waking from the dream at night delivers one from dream conditions.

Our refuge is spiritual consciousness. Our refuge is spiritual ascension. Jesus' final demonstration was called the Ascension, for he rose above all illusive testimony. *Ascension is the rising into full consciousness of Self as Spirit, of Self as God.*

Spiritual ascendency is spiritual power, delivering peace, glory, harmony, and reality. As thought harmoniously ascends the scale of being, one perceives that good alone is real and true, and good alone is Omnipresence.

Right interpretation enables one to lift thought above the dream-sense and reveals to him the spiritual body which comes with the Ascension.

Metaphysics is above physics, and spiritual ascendency is above mental practice, delivering to one the power and ability to rise above dreams and illusions, and the right and might to experience the heritage of glorified being.

Right interpretation reveals what unillumined eye doth not behold. The report that the universe is imperfect and incomplete is false, for the universe is the expression of Life, Truth, and Love and is as perfect, changeless, and immortal as is Intelligence, Life, Being, which sustains it.

It is relatively true that a mortal is not an immortal, and it is relatively true that the universe of unillumined vision is not the kingdom of heaven. One identity (Self) is ever present, whether one interprets this identity as perfect and divine, or imperfect and defective. Likewise, one universe is ever present, whether one interprets this universe as heavenly and glorious, or as material and discordant.

One Life, Truth, Love and one expression, embodiment, kingdom co-exist ceaselessly, uninterruptedly, absolutely, and finally. Casting aside erring perception and executing spiritual vision, one sees that the universe before him is none other than the kingdom of heaven and that the entity before him is none other than the perfect being.

The universe is the expression of Life and Spirit and is therefore a spiritual and perfect universe. Apprehending and recognizing the perfect universe this right way, one laborlessly and naturally enters it.

Prophets and saints have left different instruction pertaining to the way in which this kingdom of perfect harmony and immortality may be attained. Some have said that the way is by mental law—"Thou shalt not." Others have believed that the way is disclosed through tribulations, sorrows, trials. The great Master of Understanding, however, delivered the ultimatum—the kingdom of heaven is within you!

The individual himself is the way to heavenly harmony. Through *individual* perception, recognition, and acceptance of Self as God and of universe as co-existent with Self, one enters the glory of ascension, experiencing the kingdom of heaven on earth.

Jesus proclaimed to "mortals" their immortality, and on earth he established the kingdom of heaven. Truth is revealed. Perfect being and perfect universe are here; and when perfect being and perfect universe are interpreted by Absolute Science, they can be rightly understood.

The kingdom, or perfect universe, as interpreted by Jesus, is our consciousness of health, harmony, happiness, power, glory, and authority as *inherent, absolute, final, present, complete.*

Taking conscious possession of the kingdom of reality within ourselves through spiritual ascendency, we individualize infinite power and glory, and we express unlimited health, happiness and harmony.

Spiritual blessedness is based upon the action of Truth, and *instantaneous* healing is demonstrated as one sets aside mental argument, letting his enraptured sense rest in the understanding of one Presence as *All.*

Standing upon this immortal basis, one stands on reality, oneness, infinity, and his victory is assured.

The difference between the mental argument and the way of Absolute Science is that the latter has a more spiritual basis than the former. One's practical demonstration rests upon a spiritual basis as high as his understanding of it.

Permanent perfection, irresistible harmony, perpetual loveliness constitute all phenomena of being. Spiritual sense alone can understand and interpret the healing Christ. The more fully the Science of Being is understood and interpreted by the student, the higher are his demonstrations of divine power. That Absolute Science uplifts individual consciousness to a more spiritual sense of life and love, delivering health, harmony, and happiness, thousands can attest.

Absolute Science is the mighty deliverer, the all-sufficient Presence bringing out the highest phenomena of reality. Proportionately as one accepts and utilizes the understanding that his real nature is the divine Trinity, he brings out in individual experience the glorious results of this understanding.

Can we demonstrate health and glorified being instantaneously unless our own consciousness is inspired with devotion, love, and revelation? Can we give living waters to the thirsty unless our own hearts are overflowing with the miracle of divine glory?

The fire of inspiration and illumination, purifying sense with Soul, forms the coincidence of the human and divine. Through divine revelation, insight, and demonstration, the untrue view (materiality) disappears, and the reality or individual spiritual ideality—Christ—appears.

Right interpretation of the perfect universe reveals harmonious existence at hand. Looking at the ideal and interpreting it erroneously, one may call perfect creation "matter," "illusion," "counterfeit," but let it be clearly understood that the perfect Being and the universe are co-existent and eternal. The individual viewpoint, the individual interpretation of this perfect kingdom, determines for one the nature of his present individual experience.

This fact clearly and forcefully sets before all the tremendous importance that we exercise right interpretation.

Now, one may call the beautiful, glorious, heavenly universe in which we live "matter," "falsity," and he may follow this false view with another false view — the denial of matter, evil, falsity. But right interpretation delivers the insight that nothing whatever is gained by denying a thing which has no existence.

The fact is that we all live, move, and act in one perfect universe, and as we spiritually perceive and accept this marvelous certainty and individually conform our thinking and acting to this right consciousness, simultaneously our experience is harmonious, glorious, and divine.

There is no necessity to deny a material universe, *for there is no material universe.* The only universe there is for all is the one established, finished, complete, perfect kingdom.

Erroneously interpreting this finished kingdom in which all dwell — calling the good in this kingdom "evil" and the divine and glorious "material," and "changeable" — one's wrong vision prevents him from consciously experiencing the glories before him and encourages him to report a false world and a false experience.

How important then is right vision, right interpretation, and right understanding! Through the Science of Ascension we accept the facts of perfect being and perfect universe as *now* and *here*, and we discard all notion of matter, evil, and destruction. We perceive that it is useless and of no practical value whatsoever to deny evil; rather do we deny that there is evil. The same right perception is applied to matter, to sickness, to sin, and death.

Interpreting the universe rightly, we see that there is no necessity or advantage in denying matter, sickness, sin, death, for these conditions are not found in this perfect kingdom in which we are living. Who convinceth *spiritual vision* of sickness, sin, and death? Yes, the acknowledgement of the omnipresence and omnipotence of perfect changeless Being and perfect changeless experience *includes* the only right denial.

The full consciousness of perfect, continuous, and changeless being and of perfect, continuous and harmonious expression, demonstrates the nothingness of sickness, sin and evil. This spiritual action or demonstration is ascension, for here the

Self consciously perceives and expresses glory, power, perfection, and harmony.

Chapter VI

PARADISE

Paradise is within us. Our consciousness of health, joy, peace, glory, abundance, immortality is our paradise.

Spiritualization of thought and vision is the practice of prayer, and it is this practice which delivers us to the experience of peace, joy, and harmony. One is redeemed from so-called laws of the flesh as he thinks, feels, and acts in the finished kingdom. This is the way in which Soul controls sense and the way in which paradise is brought to light.

On the plane where progress appears to have an effect, our immunity from so-called evil is based upon our perception of reality and unreality and upon our ability to pray, or treat, correctly.

Having established as a foundation in our consciousness the fact that our individual identity is the actual Truth, and having accepted further that all untrue belief can be corrected by spiritual understanding, we begin to ascertain how to pray, or treat, so that deliverance from erring beliefs may be quick and certain.

How can we rise in the strength of Spirit unless we *are* Spirit? How can we execute power unless we *are* Power? How can we manifest Reality unless we *are* Reality? How can we hope to rise above discord and limitation unless we rise above the belief that the body is subject to discord and limitation? In order to laborlessly rise to our nativity in Spirit, we must apprehend our actual state (immortality) and enforce it.

How can we rise above limitation unless we are the Unlimited? How can we control erring sense unless we are Understanding? How can we remember our perfect state unless we are Intelligence? How can we hope to overcome all fear and limitation unless we perceive that *we are God-being?*

Do we not have to know that two and two are four before we can agree that two and two are not five? Must not the understanding of our actual being precede our understanding that we are not material beings and therefore are not subject to material, mortal beliefs? Most certainly.

One may take the figures 2 and 2 in adding and call the sum 5, but with a correct view one calls the sum 4. The figures 2 and 2 remaining the same, all that is undergoing change is the belief in the mind of the individual.

The figure 5 in the answer might stand for what is called a "mortal" or "human" being, and the figure 4 might stand for an immortal, spiritual being. When untrue belief operates, the answer is untrue; and when true belief or understanding operates, the answer is true.

Now we have the problem of our own existence before us. Its beginning (Genesis) is God, and its ending (Revelation) is God. The problem that is set before us is this: since God is the beginning and God is the ending — what are we?

When untrue belief operates, the answer is untrue (a mortal appearance), and when true belief operates, the answer is true (immortal Being).

When one believes that the answer to the mathematical problem is five, he writes this down; and when one believes that he is a mortal (or human) being subject to discord and limitation, he externalizes this idea. But all the time, no matter whether one is seeing rightly or wrongly, the answer is fixed, final, sure.

When one lying on his couch dreams that he is in Europe walking on foreign pavements, what manner of being is that one who is thus portrayed in the dream? In one breath we can say, "That man walking on the streets of Europe doesn't exist!" But with another view, we can trace that non-existent being back to the man upon the couch. Is this not so? We perceive one entity only — the one on the couch.

Preserving this same viewpoint and this same procedure of vision, we begin our problem with perfect, individual, spiritual being. From all about us we hear reports of pain, destruction, poverty, sorrow, disease, death. In one breath, again we can declare, "But that body is a dream body and doesn't actually exist." Yet adopting another view, we say, "That may be so, but I'll trace this mind which is reporting untruly, and I'll discover its starting place. And lo!—in looking back to the beginning, one comes face-to-face with Reality.

So we see, whichever way we look, whatever process of vision we adopt, we face the facts that the untrue belief and untrue expression are nothing and that the Truth is all.

Clear vision perceives that when the man on the couch is conscious that he is on the couch (self-conscious), he is unconscious that he is on the streets in Europe, and simultaneously the dream picture of him as being there is gone. Also, as an individual is conscious that he is God-being (Self-conscious), he is unconscious that he is a material being subject to sin, disease, and discord, and simultaneously the dream picture of sin, sickness, and death is gone.

Becoming conscious that our life and our being is wholly Spirit, God (for there is no other Life or Spirit), we are Self-conscious, and this divine process of spiritual perception and realization is called spiritual healing. Thought has now ascended, and material belief has yielded to spiritual understanding.

It is said that the stream rises as high as its source. Likewise, if we are to return to our Father, or perfect state as portrayed by the parable of the prodigal, let us see what this state is. If we are to return to perfection in consciousness, it is because we already *are* perfection. If we are to return to our God-state, it is because we *are* God-being.

If one, dreaming himself upon the streets of Europe, can rise as high as his source, and his source is the man on the couch, let him see that he is the one on the couch—and his dream is gone. If one dreaming himself in a material universe can rise as high as his source, and his source is the one Being, let him see that he is the one Being, and his dream will cease.

It seems that we are confronted with the paradox of returning to a land which we have never left. We are face-to-face with the problem of putting on the true and the putting off the untrue, when the fact is, as Jesus so simply stated:

"Ye are the light … labor not … the kingdom is within you."

"Mortals will someday assert their freedom" is prediction. Notice that it is not written "immortals," but it is written "mortals." How can a mortal assert anything at all when, as we have proven by the dream illustration, a mortal is a myth, a soul in a dream state?

The man on the couch need not assert that he is on the couch, for this is obvious and he knows it. But the mind that is dreaming itself on foreign streets—this mind wishes to return to his own home and room; this mind is tired and weary and would like rest on the comfortable couch.

The man on the couch does not need rest and repose, for he has it; but this mind in the dream feels the need of this very thing. Hence, since he feels the need, let him assert in the dream his freedom from those streets and from that country. Let him assert his freedom *in the name of the man on the couch*. And lo! the dream vanishes. There is only one presence—the man on the couch.

Now, the being of perpetual harmony does not need immortal health and glory, for he has it. But the mortal being, or the one in the dream of material existence, feels the need of this very thing; and since he it is who feels his need of health and harmony, let him assert in the dream of material existence his freedom from sickness, sin, and trouble. Let him assert his freedom in the name of Almighty God. And lo!—the dream of disease and discord vanishes. There is only one presence—Almighty God, the one Being.

Thus, while we seem to be in the dream of material existence and while we are called "mortals," we assert our freedom in the name of God, for what other name is there that shall deliver us?

This is the name written in our foreheads. This is the name of our perfect being. Joyfully we believe it. We claim it. We accept it. We love it.

When the one dreaming himself on foreign land recognizes that he is all the while on the couch, he enters his abode of peace and rest. And when mortals assert their freedom in the name of eternal Truth, they find their heritage of glory and immortality.

Treatment is the acceptance of our freedom as spiritual beings. A real being cannot be sick, and most certainly an unreal being cannot be sick. For one to know that he is real being, Spirit, is for him to experience a body that utters no complaints. This is what is meant by, "the Spirit beareth witness with our spirit" (Rom. 8:16).

When it is clear to us that our true convictions are founded upon Truth, we realize that actual Truth supports us and that Truth is all that can ever control erring sense. Hence, as we establish Truth in our consciousness we are assured of victory, and we regain our sense of paradise.

Let sense awaken to spiritual interpretation of true being. Let beliefs in limitations, bondage, personality be set aside for higher views and perceptions. The awakening to the spiritual recognition and acceptance of self as Soul is the coming of Christ to the individual, revealing paradise as a present reality.

As we advance in spiritual understanding, we perceive that right interpretation is the beginning of wisdom. Interpreting a spiritual being spiritually, one spontaneously rises to new heights wherein is disclosed to him the co-existence of Soul and universe and their unfallen spiritual perfection.

Absolute Science reveals that Omnipotence, actually enthroned in every heart, must be individually acknowledged and demonstrated. Recognizing and claiming self as Christ, God, sense is lifted to a higher basis, opening prison doors and letting in the light of glory. Lifted to the inspired consciousness of *Soul and body as one*—perfect, immaculate, all-harmonious—brings paradise on earth.

Our ascension from faith to power, from sense to glory, from cross to crown constitutes our paradise. To the awakened consciousness, sense has left the cradle of "mistification" and bondage for the crown of irresistible glory. The crown that no man taketh from us is spiritual understanding—set with the dazzling jewels of transcending love, light, and power.

The eternal verities of Being, apprehended, claimed and practiced, light our pathway with victory, delivering to us emancipation from the false sense of sin, sickness, and death, and revealing to us the glories and splendors of supernal existence.

Let us relinquish the cross, testifying to trial and tribulation, and accept the crown of enlightened understanding. Here we rest in the peace of conscious strength and power and in the practical demonstration of, "Christ in you, the hope of glory."

The recognition of the self as Soul, Spirit, Life, Truth, Love strikes the note of universal freedom, gently delivering all from erring sense and lifting them to the consciousness of Life as forever changeless, eternal, glowing, and harmonious.

Paradise is the discovery, the acceptance, and the experience of our actual entity.

If there is no selfhood apart from God, then *selfhood is God.* If there is no being separate from the One, then *all being is the One.* If body is the expression of Life, Truth, and Love, then *body is perfect, ideal, and glorious.*

The preaching of the gospel is the presentation of the changeless continuance of good, of the ever-presence of reality, glory, happiness, harmony, health on earth as in heaven.

The healing of the sick is the utilization and practice of right interpretation and insight—the delivery to the individual of his reality, his perfection, his glory.

The casting out of demons is the forsaking of false beliefs, the relinquishing of erring notions. We do not give up the body; we give up the false idea of the body. We do not give up the universe; we give up the false idea of the universe. We do not give up pleasures, companionships, activities; we give up false ideas of pleasures, companionships, activities.

The raising of the dead is the experiencing of uninterrupted peace, harmony, and immortality.

With spiritual vision we behold paradise as a reality here and now—an experience of heavenly peace, glory, harmony, delight. The preaching of the kingdom of paradise on earth is the presentation of the golden message, "Be still, and know that I am God."

Truth brings Its own peace and harmony. Truth delivers Its own joy, inspiration, and uplift. Truth can say unto darkened sense, "You cannot come into My presence without acknowledging Me as the one and only power and reality."

"And this is life eternal, that they might know thee, the only true God." This is life eternal, that we shall recognize and know our reality and identity as the only true God.

Let one vision, think, and act from the standpoint of his Lordship. If one feels that he needs quickening and illumination, that he needs the fire of Spirit, let him read the Bible and such books as contain spiritual quickening. Light kindles light, and a lighted consciousness transmits illumination.

Claiming our identity with Spirit only, we begin to have right ideas and right visions. "This sickness is for the glory of God," said Jesus with loving assurance. Rising to the consciousness of our full dominion of Spirit, we glorify our God-being. Healing is not actually healing; resurrecting is not actually resurrecting. God is changeless Reality. We are changeless Reality. Opening our vision to this supernal verity, we transcend the human steps called healing, overcoming, progressing. We see face-to-face. We discover that we have already arrived and that we are perfect *without the process of progression.*

This is the Science of Ascension, the Science of ascending above earthly states and conceptions. This is the Science of laborless acceptance and experience.

When one places himself under the action of his thought and its consequences, he hinders his advancement; but when one places himself *above* his thoughts, spontaneously he rises to greater heights.

The notion that a thought or a thing can exist independently of principle is false, and this falsity is vanquished by the realization and conscious-ness of the true facts of being. Transcending the belief in limitation and bondage, the so-called limitation and bondage disappears.

We acknowledge ourselves as free, unfettered, flawless, triumphant. We acknowledge our universe as heavenly, glorious, radiant, supernal. To know that we ourselves are Truth triumphant strikes the keynote of higher claims. As there is a strength above the strength of the body and a power above the power of the mentality, so is there a way above the way of progression.

This way is the Science of Ascension—the Science of recognizing a perfect universe and perfect being *here* and *now*. This sublime consciousness bridges over the periods called birth, age, and death, and one finds himself in heaven, the only universe, and in the full consciousness of his immortality and glory:

> I am the flame. I am the inspiration. I am the finished wholeness and completion. I am awake, alive, for evermore. Nothing can separate me from being God—"neither death, nor life, nor powers, nor things present, nor things to come."

Insight accepts the kingdom of heaven on earth. Insight reports that we are all one life, substance, being. Insight lifts us to the mount and discloses to us our real identity. Insight delivers the ultimate understanding, *the ascension*, which is the *experience* of supernal glory, harmony, and immortality.

Looking *up*, we perceive that nothing was impossible with Jesus, that nothing is impossible with us. Exalted vision discloses that there is no departure nor lapse from perfection and no return to perfection; but always, everywhere, there is one entity and one expression. As in the night one sees glowing stars, so right now, no matter how dark may seem your pathway, look up and behold this golden Light before you. Accept your real identity and love this identity. Your triumph and your redemption are here, already established, awaiting your acceptance.

One wakens from a dream by knowing that he is not in the dream. We are the dreamless, the ageless, the deathless Reality. We are the all-conquering, the self-existing, the unchangeable Christ.

Chapter VII

ROLL AWAY THE STONE

Suppose one desiring a certain precious and marvelous jewel searches and looks everywhere, but all in vain. The gem of his dream cannot be found.

Finally, one day a friend comes into his presence presenting him with a handsome velvet box. "In this box," says the friend, "you will find that for which you have long been searching. Here is the jewel of your heart. Take it, for it is yours."

Now, what is the first thing that happens to this individual? It is this. His mind is at peace. He stops longing and wondering, for he is at rest. He does not hasten to open the box. In fact, he rather delights in keeping it unopened for the moment, for behold, it is here; that which he has desired has at last come to pass.

Perhaps someone now reading these lines has problems, fears, troubles. Let this message—the Science of Ascension—be the precious jewel, the priceless treasure delivered into your hand.

There need now be no hurry about the overthrow of sin, sickness, and limitation. You can now relax and be at peace, for to the heart has come the Light and Truth, and this Light and Truth means freedom, deliverance. This Truth means laborless emancipation from a sense that is material to a sense that is divine, from a mind that is darkened to a mind that is lighted, from experience that is discordant to experience that is joyous.

The jewel is here. The mystery is unveiled. Now one sees the way; one feels the joy; one receives the glory that Infinite Consciousness has prepared for those who arise and accept the way to that heavenly city and that perfect land which in truth was never left. And into his experience comes a new heaven and a new earth, for former beliefs have passed away.

By virtue of the fact that we have abolished the belief that we are human and have accepted the understanding that we are Spirit, we are prepared to accept the glories of ascension. By virtue of the fact that we are God-being, *we cannot be sick, and we cannot die.* Our eyes now see, and our ears now hear the wonderful things that are prepared for those who accept this glorious vision.

Often it is asked why it is that some students apprehend and accept advanced ideas of Truth readily and easily. Others, apparently equally as eager and earnest, do not accept the presentation but instead hold tenaciously to differing views and concepts.

The process of individual acceptance may be made clear by the following illustration: suppose that a party of friends enters a new and beautifully furnished residence to examine its style, furniture, art, etc. In this party are an electrician, an artist, a musician, as well as children of varying ages.

They all enter this spacious and luxuriously furnished home. Do you see the musician giving his attention first of all to the tapestries or to the floors or the decorations of the ceiling? Indeed not. He finds the grand piano, and, for the time, this absorbs his whole attention. And the artist — is he, too, stationed at the piano? Why, already he is wandering from room to room, engrossed with the etchings and paintings. The electrician examines the latest style of electric fixtures and is interested in the radio. The children amuse themselves with games and books. Each adult seeks that which particularly captures his attention.

Now, everything about this group of people is just as it should be at that moment, is it not?

Each one is following a certain mental inclination and culture, and each one is finding pleasure and satisfaction at his particular point of attention.

It is quite like this with the great numbers of people who study the Bible and who study metaphysical works and messages. We find books, written by highly specialized minds, setting forth verses from the Bible to prove that Jesus was the son of man. On the same shelf with these books are others, written by equally respected minds, setting forth verses from the same Bible to prove that Jesus was the Son of God, and actually God Himself. Year after year, century after century, new books of such character are being published.

It is like this when it comes to the study of metaphysical science. It seems that from the same textbook variously different ideas are received and promulgated. It simply means that one expresses himself according to his individual state of consciousness.

The child pursues life in a different direction from the adult, and each one absorbs from books and teachings that which corresponds to his present view of life and being. This is the reason why one can seemingly find in the Bible whatever will support his belief, no matter which side of the message he had adopted as his viewpoint. The Bible furnishes this paradox.

Jesus stated, "All power is given unto me in heaven and in earth"; yet, "Of mine own self I can do nothing."

Another Biblical paradox: "The flesh profiteth nothing" (John 6:63); "Flesh cannot inherit the kingdom of God" (1 Cor. 15:50). Yet, "All flesh shall see the salvation of God" (Luke 3:6); "That the life also of Jesus might be made manifest in our mortal flesh" (2 Cor. 4:11).

Another: "I form the light, and create darkness: I make peace, and create evil: I, the Lord, do all these things" (Isa. 45:7); yet, "God is light, and in him is no darkness at all" (1 John 1:5); "Thou art of purer eyes than to behold evil" (Hab. 1:13).

The one of insight is not dismayed by these seeming contradictions. Climbing the ladder of life, we choose what we shall see and believe. But there comes a time when we no longer choose, no longer separate, no longer adopt certain specific forms of beliefs, for now the paradox is plain to us—we see on all sides, and we reconcile all as one.

We can now understand another's view no matter where he stands upon the ladder. Also, we can show him the next step ahead. To one of exalted vision, all views blend into one great reality, and at last one can say understandingly, "There is no evil."

A child has the right to childhood, and one in his study of life has a perfect right to think and act according to his vision. Indeed, what else can he do? Therefore, during the transitional period wherein one is choosing, selecting, balancing, arguing, separating, and dividing, he acts according to his unfolding vision. He is seeing two factors, two sides to life, and he is choosing between them.

But when he has reached a certain peak of vision—perhaps slowly, perhaps swiftly—he perceives the paradox, and he exclaims with the prophet, "The darkness and the light are both alike." From then on, he commences to perceive *oneness*. Wherever he looks, whatever he reads— in the office, in the home, on the screen, in the stars—lo! everything speaks to him of the *one* Life, the *one* Being, the *one* Expression.

He sees now why it is that over the world is heard a word echoing from the super-plane—the word *cooperation*. Does this not mean oneness, agreement, unity? Certainly it does. Down through the ages it has been eternally sounding, "Let there be light!" Multitudes are hearing as they never heard before, and earnest and eager attention is focused on peace, on harmony, on service, on love, on oneness.

"That which hath been is now; and that which is to be hath already been" (Eccles. 3:15). Every good thing that seems coming to us is already here. It is coming to individual recognition, that is all. It is being apprehended by individual consciousness. In reality it has been from eternity, but now it is appearing to us individually. This is the way in which "creation" is finished; yet creation is constantly and eternally appearing to individual recognition.

With the dawning in consciousness of this view of oneness and indivisibility, one gently rises from a mortal, limited state of thinking to a free, immortal state of understanding. With this heavenly vision there appears the new earth; for always, corresponding expression accompanies ascending states of consciousness.

Verily, O Glorious Reality, Thy kingdom is coming—*is here*—on earth as it is in heaven.

Swiftly comes the end of darkness when light arrives. Swiftly over all the face of the earth comes the end of separation, division, opposition, ignorance— for the Light of Reality is here. Illumination consumes all misunderstanding and the King of Love and Glory is enthroned in hearts, in social groups, in nations.

Day by day, the whole world is echoing back the song of angels:

"Glory to God in the highest, and on earth peace, good will toward men." —Luke 2:14

Of what advantage is it to have a Selfhood that is God—almighty, unlimited, all-powerful, all-glorious—if we do not let this One *live* in us; if we do not let this One *shine* in us; if we do not let this One *act* in us?

To realize freedom, authority, let us accept and practice the One Presence as *All*. In this way, that which has seemed false in our minds will be transcended—swallowed up by the good in our own true nature.

As we perceive the allness of the One and the oneness of the All, we can say, "Heaven is here;

the desert blossoms as the rose; the lion and the lamb express the same being."

Ever it is *I*, the divine Mind, the Jesus Christ-Self, which speaketh, saying,

> *I* am whole. *I* am perfect. *I* am wonderful. *I* am glorious. *I* am victorious. *I* am All, and besides Me there is no other authority.

Always there is a way of escape because of the mental nature of limitation. For example: A caterpillar cannot fly. But suppose he should wish that he might fly; of what avail would his wish be, since it is not the nature of the caterpillar to fly? There is a path, however, a way for him unseen by reason. There is a way of deliverance. Let that entity put on (accept) the butterfly—then he can fly.

Now, the human being wishes to be perfect, to be free, to be well and divine. But it is not in the nature of a material being to be perfect, to be glorious, to be free and divine. Yet there is a solution; there is a way of fulfillment. The way is that of Absolute Science.

Let the so-called mortal put off the state of false belief for the state of understanding. Let him emerge from material belief into spiritual ascension—"from matter into spirit"—then automatically he is glorious; he is divine; he is free.

A butterfly need not crawl. Neither need, nor can, an immortal being function in sickness, sin, and death. Behold the Light. Behold the Way. Behold the Science of Ascension.

The God to whom we look, to whom we turn for deliverance, is verily our own true Being. The God who healeth and redeemeth and saveth is verily the Self of Jesus, the Self of You, the Self of Me, the one and only Self—one God; one Totality.

It has been stated that we must translate the universe back into Spirit; that we must interpret spiritual things spiritually. For instance, we are to perceive that *we* are the divine Mind and that we manifest all which comprises the infinitude of Truth.

Jesus, while in human form, demonstrated the spiritual revelation of atonement, resurrection, and ascension. As life is spiritually interpreted, material sense is put off for spiritual Science. This transition from a lower or human sense of life to a new and higher sense presents the way of fulfillment through earthly development. Jesus' nativity being a spiritual sense of a spiritual world, naturally his mission was to interpret the spiritual universe spiritually.

Inspiration is the Light which illumines the darkness and reveals to us that, like Jesus, our nativity is Spirit, Soul. In the dark hour, let this inspiration shine, for it is *inspiration* which individualizes infinite power, sweeping aside clouded sense as the breeze sweeps away mist.

125

Inspiration proceeds from a consciousness which believes in *almighty* Truth, a consciousness which speaks *imperatively* from the basis of faith and understanding.

What "stone" or obstacle can withstand Omnipotence? When one has the living Fire, he fears nothing, for this living Flame is a law unto Itself and is absolute authority.

Whatever seems an obstacle in our path can be rolled away by insight and inspiration. The fire of courage, certainty, power born of spiritual inspiration is the flaming sword which turns every way to establish life as irresistible, triumphant, victorious, and supreme.

The "new tongue" accompanies right interpretation. As one translates things into ideas, and ideas into Soul, he needs a higher expression to convey his advanced understanding and make practical the commands of Jesus.

Every advancing period delivers a higher and clearer interpretation of Being. As the vision of Truth becomes more fully interpreted and practiced, individuals will more clearly apprehend their original and absolute state of being. They will rise naturally and easily to the mount of revelation, crowning earth with irresistible glory. Thought will soar above false beliefs to triumphant freedom and to the understanding and experience of ineffable love, light, and glory.

Human experience gives us plenty of opportunity to express that spiritual dominion which was enthroned in us in the beginning. Exercising this dominion, one advances rapidly in spiritual vision and spiritual revelation.

The view from the mountain peak seems quite different from the view in the valley. Looking from the mount of spiritual vision, one sees that the heavenly kingdom has come to earth, that perfection, glory, harmony, immortality are established without beginning or ending and that this being is forever perfectly expressed and manifested.

Looking from the valley, one perceives progress, advancement, regeneration. One perceives that seeds become plants and that mortals become immortals through spiritualization and regeneration.

From the mount of vision one views the universe clearly and interprets it truly, while from the valley one looks through mistaken sense and interprets the perfect world imperfectly, untruly, materially.

Seeing the perfect universe through a veil or mist, one sees it by degrees, step by step ascending as the veil is lifted. For instance, when healing takes place, it appears as though the body had changed from sickness to health, and when one manifests life more abundantly, it appears as though he were immortalizing the body.

The fact is, however, that no one can immortalize his body, for the reason that this act has already been accomplished. The body is perfect now, and this perfect body is recognized and understood when rightly viewed.

Roll away the stone of erring vision, for "Behold, I make all things new" (Rev. 21:5). Into the mind there comes a new sense, a feeling of joyous inspiration and courage, for now it is seen that while there is nothing to be done or outwardly accomplished, there is an inner viewpoint which shall be attained. It is as this correct viewpoint is attained that we express the Truth in our daily experience.

There are not two beings, one spiritual and the other material, nor are there two worlds, one perfect and the other imperfect. Looking with clear vision, one interprets all things spiritually, perfectly. Looking through mistaken sense, one reports spiritual reality falsely, calling the spiritual being a material being and speaking of perfect universe as a material world.

Now that insight is here, we joyously accept it, and we love life, and we love all the activities of a perfect universe.

As one gains a clearer and clearer view of perfect Life and Its perfect expression, it seems as though he were actually immortalizing and perfecting his body. He is perfecting his *viewpoint*, that is all; he is establishing himself on the mountain peak and is seeing life spiritually, instead of dwelling in the valley and interpreting life materially.

Proportionately as one widens his horizon does he more correctly view and interpret perfect complete being and perfect complete universe. No change ever takes place in perfect established being or in perfect established expression. Our prerogative is to know this sublime reality and to apprehend this fact of being.

It is clearly seen that Jesus, while on earth and "in the flesh," viewed a perfect universe and that he continually called this kingdom to the attention of those around him. He also saw perfect expression as ever-present. His instantaneous healings prove this fact.

Now, when one individual is perceiving Life and Its expression from the mountain peak, and another individual is viewing Life and Its expression from the valley, their reports seem opposed to each other. The one on the peak reports beauty, harmony, glory, perfection, while he in the valley reports discord, sickness, sin, bondage.

Let it be very clearly grasped and fixed in consciousness that the discord is not opposing the harmony; that sickness is not the opposite of health, nor is bondage at war with freedom. It is a mistake to let mind accept the notion of separation, opposition, warfare, for nothing of this sort is present anywhere.

Let us adopt the new tongue, revising our vocabulary and striking out words which do not harmonize to the divine viewpoint. Why waste time and glory in discussing what isn't true? Why not hasten to the marriage feast already prepared and eat and drink with our risen Lord? In proportion as one rises above mistaken sense and its viewpoint, he finds himself on the mountain peak, understanding that the universe is *one* and that whether one visions from the peak or from the valley, what he sees is altogether a matter of consciousness.

Death is not the opposite of life, nor is evil the opposite of good, for the simple reason that one is *ever*-present while the other is always illusion. If you enter a dimly lighted room and mistake a pedestal for an intruder, would it not be practicing absurdity to declare the intruder the opposite of the pedestal?

In Omnipresence there are no opposites. This is right vision. This is the view beheld from the mountaintop. Never does the material expression contradict the spiritual reality; never does earth contradict heaven. Nothing can contradict Reality, for Reality is *all*, and Reality is forever established.

One ceases to mention "materiality" and "evil" when he apprehends and accepts completeness and uninterrupted fullness as *one* Presence now and here. Using the new tongue, erring expressions drop away naturally and without taking thought.

"We shall see him as he is" (1 John 3:2). It is an established certainty that we shall perceive perfect being and perfect universe as they are; that drinking of the living waters, we shall see face-to-face.

As mistaken sense fades out, one perceives reality more clearly. Misinterpreting this process of vision, however, one erringly speaks of reality as physical healing and physical improvement. It should be known that we do not restore the body; instead, we restore the *sense* of it; we restore the point of vision. This is accomplished by calmly and trustingly declaring that good is ever-present, that there are no opposites; that one Presence and one experience are forever here and with us.

Every living thing enjoys freedom. Birds and animals and high-souled men love great forests and unwalled spaces. All living things delight in freedom, because Life Itself is freedom. All living things cling to life. No matter how many years one has been in this world, even at the end he wishes to remain in it—to stay a little longer, to prolong the time with loved ones. Why is that? Because Soul cannot consider destruction. Life knows no such thing as death. Life and Its individual activity cannot be separated.

We give ourselves to the One, and there remains no sense of personality, no notion of separation. It is because the One is our life and is our heart that we can never be entirely satisfied with the joys and pleasures of this world. Do we not see men continually searching after happiness, always eager to have greater abundance, never quite satisfied but always seeking just a little further ahead? Now, one may believe that he is seeking pleasure in material things — greater abundance of wealth, nearer and dearer companionships—but all the while it is Truth that he is seeking. He is seeking his heart, his treasure, *himself.*

Now, in one language this is called evolution and in another language is called progress. But rising above languages, we see that one shall find himself; that one shall meet his own glory and shall know his own divinity. One will never be satisfied with less than *All,* because his nature is the Unlimited, the Eternal, the Infinite. It may seem to him that he seeks companionship, wealth, amusement, but even though he may know it not, he seeks the Unchangeable. He seeks the Unlimited, the Infinite, the Eternal.

Seeking his perfection, his Reality, he will never desist until he finds it—until he comes face-to-face with his own glory.

"As for me, I shall be satisfied when I awake with thy likeness" (Ps. 17:15).

We naturally love all things beautiful, lovely, desirable; not really for things themselves, as one may believe, but for the Self. The Self is beauty and so loves beauty. We desire wealth, unlimited abundance of all things, not for the sake of wealth itself, that we may accumulate or hoard it, but for the Self. The Self is the eternal wealth of joy and satisfaction.

We love people, friends, companions, relatives, not that we may attach ourselves to them, but we love them because we see in them the Self. The Self knows that It is universal and omnipresent and so constantly and continually seeks to express and embody Itself. The Source of all joy, peace, satisfaction, glory is Us—the Self.

We are here for a greater destiny than to function in time and space. There is something in us which urges us ever up and on, which promises that we shall be conscious of our *omnipresence* and be instantly wherever we wish to be; that we shall become conscious of our *omniscience* and have instantly revealed to us any particular knowledge that we may desire at the moment; that we shall be conscious of our *omnipotence* and merely speak the

Word and it shall come to pass; that we shall become conscious of our *immortality* and live forever.

The Christ eternally breathes upon us the message of our everlasting glory, wonder, power, majesty, and immortality.

If we feel burdened by matter and mind, by belief in the hardness of human problems, we rise up and sing; we take our hymn book and raise our voice in song and praise. One cannot sing long without the feeling that he is lifted above his problem. Song inspires and lifts up the mind so that seeming troubles begin to manifest less of proportion, less of weight, and soon they appear smaller and farther away.

We sing until we *feel* the answer within us, feel the warmth and the glory of peace and power. Throughout the Bible one may find that there are many examples of quick deliverance and emancipation from erring belief through song and praise.

"Roll away the stone!" Sing and praise Life for Its wonderful freshness and ever-restoring fairness and loveliness. Praise Intelligence for Its omnipotence and dominion. Praise Love for Its ever-flowing affection and forgiveness. Praise Truth for Its outpouring abundance and Its wealth of living ideas. Open the heart and let it rejoice in song; let it come into its own, the kingdom of supernal delight.

Song brings a quickening, a melting down of false beliefs in the mind, a breaking away of clouds, a rending of the tomb of ignorance. *Roll ye away the stone!*

Whatever seems a tomb enclosing one in the delusion of darkness and night, his song can roll the stone away. Jesus, coming to the tomb of his friend, issued the order, "Roll away the stone!" Now, he who found it possible to reproduce the presence of Lazarus, so that he walked forth in triumphant glory, could certainly have caused the stone to roll away without assistance other than the authority of the Word alone.

Jesus saw something, however, that these people could now do for themselves, something that would symbolize the rolling away of a stone of much greater importance. In the midst of every individual is this all-knowing Power which can roll away the stone or seeming obstacle.

Those who say that they have never felt the Presence, heard the Voice, or seen the Light have nevertheless read the words, "Believe in me." Begin at once to believe in this omnipresent Christ and begin at once to accept this Christ *as your own Self*. Accepting, believing, watching, praising, one reaches understanding which is able to do all things for him.

We are conscious of our hands and feet—why should we not be conscious of our Life and Soul?

Now, this living Soul has been called the Christ, the superconscious mind, the Father, and many other terms. But the underlying meaning is the same—*it is one Being; it is one Reality.*

Learn the Science of Ascension and *be free*. Through the understanding and practice of this Science, you will control error with Truth, sense with Soul, and belief with Understanding.

As one sees that he himself is the Trinity, that he himself is the Light and the Way, he becomes fearless and free.

How can one help but receive that which is his very own; that which ever remains awaiting his recognition and acceptance? From beginning to end, from eternity to eternity, he is destined to come into realization that the kingdom of God is his and that his actual being is the One.

Ascension is the exercise of one's inherent glory. Ascension is the drinking of living water and the partaking of heavenly bread.

It is predestined from eternity that at some time in the experience of every individual, false sense will be found unreal and untrue, and true Consciousness will be found complete and ever-present.

Revelation brings all things to our remembrance, transcending the evidence of the material senses and translating sense and language back into their original tongue and substance.

Let us not be selfish with this glorious understanding and light, but let us give it freely to the universe. Let us rejoice to see the spreading of Truth, no matter who speaks It or what avenue opens for Its expression. When we can look upon everyone as ourself, blessing all efforts to bring the kingdom of heaven on earth, then we are *practicing* our vision and are beholding the divine Science which has rolled away the stone from the sepulchre of our Lord.

Let us say,

> All the good I ever thought, all the good I ever said or did, this good was not mine but was Thine. Let the universe take it. Let all who will, take it—for what is Thine is universal, having no attachment, having no will but the will of universal love and brotherhood.

So shall we receive freely, even as we give freely. And the good that we do, the wisdom that we speak, will be so wonderful, so great in light and glory, that our personal self will be entirely lost sight of, and the impersonal and universal Christ will reign supreme. Then indeed are we glorified. Then indeed are we prepared to behold the Creation which is perfect and good and which can be seen face-to-face.

Discovering the power of insight to break the dream of false sense, *we spiritualize thought and action,* demonstrating the unreality of sin, sickness, and discord.

A material sense of life is all that has to be relinquished, and this action takes place automatically as one perceives and accepts his actual Being and his actual heritage. Material sense yields to the Science of Ascension in proportion as one learns and practices the radiance of his free, flawless, and triumphant Self.

The Science of Reality wipes away tears, lifts off shackles, and delivers glory, power, insight, and triumph.

Sickness, sin, limitation, bondage exist only as false sense, and as this darkened sense is controlled with the light of spiritual perception and understanding, such limitation and bondage cease, and one finds himself free, unfettered, and harmonious.

The power of light over darkness is universally accepted and utilized. Likewise, the "new tongue," explaining the power of enlightened spiritual sense over mistaken deluded belief, is rapidly coming into a wider recognition and acceptance.

The foundation of spiritual healing is Truth, insight, understanding. As one attains a mind in harmony with Truth, he *laborlessly* experiences a body governed and controlled by harmony.

Every step we take spiritually places us more firmly and surely in the realm of conscious joy, glory, and happiness. The emancipation of our bodies from sickness, our minds from fear, and our lives from discord follows the perception, understanding, and acceptance of our being as the Unlimited, Adorable, and Eternal.

In the Science of Omnipotence there is no "Lo, here! or lo, there!" but steadily, firmly, we keep our mind on the fact that there is but *one* Substance, *one* Power, *one* Life, and *one* Being.

When spiritual perception reaches Truth, then error is subdued and it disappears. The human mind advancing above itself toward sublime Reality relinquishes the mistaken and transient view for spiritual perception and divine consciousness.

Thus, as mind accepts spiritual understanding it rises above all falsity, and the divine Consciousness is found to be the only Mind, Intelligence, and Actuality. Then appear a new heaven and a new earth, and former views and things will have passed away.

Sin, sickness, death are unsustained by Truth and will disappear and be swallowed up in spiritual Truth and Reality—in victory, ascension, and triumph.

Revelation and illumination, transmitted by spiritual Consciousness, correct erring sense and erring belief, transforming earth with triumphal glory.

Because the One is all being, and all being is the One, a realization of this fact will deliver us from evil and will open our vision to behold the spiritual phenomena of divine Reality.

Consciousness, held in a false sense of existence, will be uplifted, purified, and elevated, either by ascension or by the progressive human steps, until all come into the knowledge of Reality and rise superior to limited sense and existence.

Accept the joys and glories of your real being. True understanding will roll away the stone and will open for you the door to supernal delights.

You can achieve all good, all joy, and all happiness. Seek first the understanding of spiritual reality (the kingdom of heaven), then the abundance of infinite glories, pleasures, and harmonies will be showered upon you.

As the heart accepts the sublime message that individual being is Being individualized, under the law of love, the law of the Christ presence, consciousness is then released from its fears and darkness, and spontaneously it rises to behold the spotless glory of spiritual being, spiritual body, and spiritual universe.

It has been said that all spiritual teaching in this world may be rightly grouped under three headings. The first heading is: *I am His.* Here God is thought of in the third person. One talks *about* God. One sings *about* God. One says, "I am His" as though God were a great way off.

The second group or heading is this: *I am Thine.* God is now being brought closer to the individual. God is not spoken of or about, but God is spoken *to.* God now becomes nearer and nearer. God hears and answers prayer.

In the third position the veil of duality is torn completely away. Oneness now holds the vision, and the cry is: *"I am Thou."* Now "mine" and "Thine" are the same. *The One* is recognized, acknowledged, and accepted as *All.*

Thus, shall we not all find that one after another we have taken just these three positions in our seeming journey from sense to Soul? *I am His! I am Thine! I am Thou!*

> Arise, shine; thy light is come;
> The glory of the Lord is upon thee.
> —Isaiah 60:1

FINIS

141

About the Author

Lillian DeWaters was born in 1883 and lived in Stamford, Connecticut. She grew up with a Christian Science background and in her early teens began to study metaphysics and on that same day to seriously study the Bible. "It was from the Bible that I learned to turn from all else to God direct …. What stood out to me above all else was the fact presented, that when they turned to God they received Light and Revelation; they walked and talked with God; and they found peace and freedom."

She published three books while actively within the Christian Science organization, and then in 1924 she had an awakening experience when it was as though a veil was parted and Truth was revealed to her. From that point she began to receive numerous unfoldments which led to her separation from the Christian Science organization.

She created her own publishing company and became a prolific writer with over 30 books published in 15 languages. She was a well-known teacher who taught regularly at the Waldorf Astoria in New York, and she was sought after as a healer throughout the world.

All of her books were written based on direct unfoldments of Absolute Truth, and each book reveals specific Truth that serious students will immediately recognize and treasure.

Ma Shaw's Wars

Dennis Shaw

747 4527

Published by Dennis Shaw
Publishing partner: Paragon Publishing, Rothersthorpe
First published 2011
© Dennis Shaw 2011

ISBN 978-1-907611-79-7

Book design, layout and production management by Into Print
www.intoprint.net
01604 832149

Printed and bound in UK and USA by Lightning Source

Contents

Chapter 1: This country is at war with Germany 7

Chapter 2: Some enemy aircraft will inevitably get through 17

Chapter 3: Wave after wave of Nazi bombers, some 350 in total, droned over the city 23

Chapter 4: We could have been burned alive 35

Chapter 5: Their world fell in on top of them, it was hell on earth 44

Chapter 6: No designer stubble for Frank Simms Shaw 50

Chapter 7: A fiery halo above...it would have been beautiful had it not been so deadly. 64

Picture Gallery

Chapter 8: Had I panicked I would have drowned 75

Chapter 9: Some of the bloodiest battles of the war took place there 85

Chapter 10: We would discuss our sins....so that we had something to confess 96

Chapter 11: The news pouring in, the urgency of everyone involved, the vibrancy... 107

Chapter 12: You were bawled at, goaded, insulted, belittled 119

Chapter 13: I decided I could take liberties 124

Chapter 14: I would have imagined our mom, as if in some great musical hall in the sky 131

Author's Preface

The urge to write the following pages first stirred when there was widespread publicity to the 70th anniversary of the outbreak of World War 2. Around that time war anniversaries had started to create an increasing interest among the public, possibly sparked by the conflict in Iraq and Afghanistan.

TV shots of coffins, containing the body of another of 'our lads', coming home from faraway places has been a shock to generations who have known mostly peace, unlike my late mother who for years seemed mostly to see only war.

It reminded me, more and more, that she had lived through not one, but two, world wars and lost loved ones in the battlefield in WW1...that brother Jim had landed at Normandy and won the Military Medal in helping defeat Germany in WW2....that another brother Tony and I, the last of a combined family of ten children, had been evacuated twice yet still lived through many of the horrors of the Birmingham Blitz.

Another thought that influenced the writing of the book was that in being part of a large and expanding family....(father of four children, grandfather of eight, great grandfather of three, at the last count, with more on the way), I maybe had some responsibility to offer future generations of this family, and others, an insight into what life was like for us at a time of global conflict.

Finally, the ingredient that clinched it: since I've been earning a living as a journalist for more than 60 years now, not only am I, at nearly 78, one of that dying breed. I'm one of a smaller dying breed who have the capacity, the experience and the desire to put words on paper. So that's what I've done.

Along the way I decided that, to make it (hopefully) readable, and not just a boring family history, I would attempt to write it as though it were a novel even though everything recounted here is as true and accurate as I can make it. Yes, it is dramatised here and there a little, but there's no 'spin', nothing has been invented. My aim has been simply to make the story of an ordinary women's extraordinary life, easy and interesting to read.

I hope it works.

Dennis Shaw, January 2011.

Acknowledgements

The author acknowledges the use of the following sources in his research carried out for the compilation of Ma Shaw's Wars: Cunningham family genealogy by Graham Taylor; BSA blitz details from WW2 People's War website; Jim Norton's Military Medal citation and battle description (Worcestershire Regiment website); Wikipedia encyclopedia for Birmingham bombing, Spitfire factory and other blitz facts.

'Wage war against a monstrous tyranny...'

"We have before us an ordeal of the most grievous kind.

"We have before us many, many long months of struggle and of suffering.

"You ask, what is our policy? I can say: It is to wage war, by sea, land and air, with all our might and with all the strength that God can give us; to wage war against a monstrous tyranny, never surpassed in the dark, lamentable catalogue of human crime. That is our policy.

"You ask, what is our aim? I can answer in one word: It is victory, victory at all costs, victory in spite of all terror, victory, however long and hard the road may be; for without victory, there is no survival."

Winston Churchill's message to the nation after King George V1 had invited him to become Prime Minister, in succession to Neville Chamberlain, at the outbreak of World War 2.

Ma Shaw's Wars

Chapter 1

'...this country is at war with Germany.'

We all gathered round the radio on that historic morning, September 3, 1939. My brother Tony was eight. I was six. With us were our Mother and Father, Margaret and Frank Shaw, and other members of our large and complicated family.

Around Britain similar groups were assembled, anxiously awaiting a special broadcast at 11.15 am, by the Prime Minister, Neville Chamberlain. Young though we were Tony and I knew what the message would be.

Adolf Hitler and his German High Command had long since begun their goose-stepping march across whole swathes of mainland Europe using military power allied to their ambition to produce a master race as the excuse to crush nation after nation into terrified submission.

Even as kids, myself at school for little more than a year, we knew that war was on the way. On the radio, in the newspapers, and in the newsreels at the cinema, the talk had been of little else for months on end. Even so, when the confirmation arrived, Britain became a nation in shock.

In sad and laborious words, spoken with leaden tongue, the country's beleaguered political leader told everyone the news that they fully expected, but dreaded to hear:

"This morning the British Ambassador in Berlin handed the German Government a final note stating that unless we heard from them by eleven o'clock that they were prepared at once to withdraw their troops from Poland, a state of war would exist between us." The words fell mournfully to the ears of listeners paralysed with fear for the future.

"I have to tell you that no such understanding has been received and that consequently this country is at war with Germany," he added.

As the speech ended, and the wireless became momentarily silent, adults old enough to remember all that had happened 20-odd years earlier gave a monumental, collective shudder. The notorious ' fourteen-eighteen war' as it was known , had been described as 'The War to End all Wars' but, as fate was to demonstrate, it was no such thing. This one would be longer. And, certainly on the home front, bloodier.

From the firesides people, numb with foreboding, wandered out into the streets wondering what would happen next. 'Oh! My god we're at war. Not again...!' Neighbours poured out exclamations of horror to each other, wives and mothers contemplating their menfolk being sucked into the latest murderous lunacy.

Later Neville Chamberlain's words were endorsed, again on radio, by King George V1 with a speech that was to achieve greater fame in early 2011 by the widespread showing of **The King's Speech,** a film that achieved international acclaim. The public at large did not know at the time of his struggle against a serious stutter in order to be able to deliver a message that began:

"In this grave hour, perhaps the most fateful in our history, I send to every household of my peoples, both at home and overseas, this message, spoken as if I were able to cross your threshold and speak to you myself.

"For the second time in the lives of most of us we are at war. Over and over again we have tried to find a peaceful way out of the differences between ourselves and those who are now our enemies. But it has been in vain. We have been forced into a conflict. For we are called, with our allies, to meet the challenge of a principle which, if it were to prevail, would be fatal to any civilised order in the world..."

"So what happens next ?" When will the Germans invade our shores? Tony and I looked into the skies for German aircraft and to the end of the street, wondering when German soldiers and tanks would appear, trying to be excited but scared almost out of our skins. We had seen World War 1 films at the cinema. This time it was for real.

What we couldn't possible have known, or even taken in had we been told, were the memories that must have been racing through Our Mom's mind as Neville Chamberlain's sombre announcement ended. They were memories too awful to contemplate, as she was reminded of what was to follow the last time that war broke out, in 1914.

Killed in action September 26, 1915: Husband, 524 Private Edward 'Teddy' Norton, Royal Warwickshire Regiment. Wounded near Arras, died on way from battle to field hospital.

Killed in action June 28, 1918: Older brother, 19367 Lance Corporal, Edward, John 'Teddy' Cunningham, Royal Gloucestershire Regiment. Second battle of the Somme.

Killed in action September 15, 1918: Younger brother, 45601 Private James Thomas 'Jim' Cunningham, Hampshire Regiment. Attacking Germany's Hindenburg Line.

Mom was never even going to see her first husband's grave. She never went abroad in her life. It was nearly 90 years later that two of her sons, Jim and Tony, found it in a war cemetery near the village of Arras, the vicinity in which he died, behind the front line, of wounds sustained in the sharp end of the battles. On the gravestone it simply said: "Never forgotten by loving wife and children. Also sister Ada."

Now the human sacrifices are to be demanded again. What new agonies are in store this time ?

The Cunningham family were among the masses of Irish folk who had fled the abject poverty of rural Ireland in the middle of the 1800s as, throughout the nineteenth century, some four million Irish were calculated to have died through malnutrition and the like. The Cunninghams were of similar ilk to those featured in the famous film *Titanic,* families who were impoverished, economic migrants heading for America and of whom my mother was a 'third generation' immigrant.

Mom's parents were second generation settlers who found sanctity among the back-to-back houses in Birmingham's inner ring, near the famous Jewellery Quarter. With small industry in full flow jobs could be had in the surrounding factories and foundries where, though more affluent than in the potential starvation of Ireland, life was tough and uncompromising.

The men either worked or drank and the womenfolk were more or less mere skivvies. Mom was said to be a 'very pretty' appealing little girl with lovely, wavy hair who was known by everyone as Dolly because she looked like one. There was neither radio nor TV, cinema was in its infancy, motor cars were for the very rich and, for the poor, and the non-religious, pubs stood alone as the main means of escape from poverty and the greyness of industrial Birmingham's inner ring. Back-to-back living meant life in the raw, with as many as six houses packed into one yard, all accessed by the same entry from the street.

Neighbours had to use the same outside lavatory with torn up newspapers for toilet roll and no facilities for hand washing. Unless the landlord was thoughtful enough to attach a bolt to the inside of the door, or one of the neighbours took it upon themselves to install one, privacy could only be obtained by singing out loud whilst installed on the throne or by evacuating the bowels or bladder with one foot outstretched towards the door.

Bathrooms were merely posh facilities for the upper classes so, for what passed as personal hygiene, was achieved by means of a tin bath in the kitchen occasionally or a trip to the public baths to ensure that printer's ink, or any other even more embarrassing stains, were regularly removed from around people's private parts. Communal smells and lavatorial sound effects were part of the way of life for the poor and yet, among and between many of the families, dignity and respect were upheld. So were standards of behaviour.

Housewives scrubbed the front step almost daily. They swept their own patch of the yard, cleaned the windows, made a big show of wash day every Monday, just to show the neighbours that they were dutiful wives and mothers. Pride was at stake. Otherwise the tongues would wag in the yard and you could be bracketed with those others who lived more squalid lives in areas where frightful slums developed.

Only a few snippets passed down by word of mouth give clues to what it was really like for young Dolly but it's not hard to imagine. Her father, like all the men, probably drank a lot. Her mother was described to me as 'typically Irish' and unyieldingly Roman Catholic.

Sons were excused if they brawled outside the local boozer, sowed their wild oats and swore like troopers in the trenches. Boys will be boys, they said. But with girls it was different. They had to stay at home, help with the housework, stay out of the pubs, remain steadfastly pure for when the right man came along. Sex education was virtually non-existent.

Whatever it was that made babies, girls were expected to wait until they were safely married before they found out. Then, according to the Roman Catholic code of the day, the wife should be stoically ready for when her man was ready to indulge his marital rights and she should willingly do her duty, most likely when he came out of the pub. No birth control.

Just more babies....Lie back and think of England. Only tarts enjoy it...

Those born out of wedlock were 'illegitimate' to put it politely or 'bastards' to use the more popular vernacular. My mother told us more than once that when she got married she knew little worth knowing about how babies were created.

My mother had three brothers, Teddy, Jack and James, and two sisters, Ellen and Annie, living in Princip Street. Her mother Margaret was from a McKiernan family who, like the Cunninghams, had fled the frightful poverty of mid-19th century Ireland. Mom's father, a factory worker, died at 41 in 1903 with tuberculosis when she was only ten. So now, with the main breadwinner gone, my widowed grandmother couldn't cope with her six kids so mom and her elder sister Annie, were sent to a branch of the Cunningham family in Shrewsbury.

John Cunningham, senior, my great, great grandfather, was described as a 'Ride Officer' a job believed to be that of a Customs and Excise Officer, on horseback, who patrolled the immigrant route as his fellow Irish folk arrived from Dublin and headed by horse-drawn coach to the first stopping off place from Holyhead, namely Shrewsbury.

He was probably relatively well paid and so, for a while, life was better for the two girls. They were introduced to theatre and both were found to have pleasant singing voices. It sounds an innocent enough activity, yet it caused deep, deep divisions with their mother and older brother, Teddy. Being third generation immigrants, and having been reared in first Birmingham then Shrewsbury, the two sisters thought of themselves as 'English'. In contrast, their mother was profoundly Irish, with her roots in County Cork. Almost certainly she was inherently resentful of the way her mother country had been treated by British governments.

Although having escaped across the Irish sea, she proudly maintained her heritage, staunchly a Roman Catholic, the broadest of Irish brogues, a tendency to wear a cap and smoke a pipe, like a man, maybe to the embarrassment of my mother who wanted to be a typically English young woman. With such diverse cultural divides it's not surprising that they didn't get on too well.

My Grannie Margaret had no time for what she regarded as 'loose or irresponsible behaviour' and her oldest son, Edward, had the same strict outlook, but probably only where girls were concerned. With his father gone he took on the role of the senior male in the family. Like his mother, he disapproved of his two young sisters being encouraged to continue with singing, possibly in public and to enjoy popular musical hall songs, some of them regarded as too racy for Roman Catholic young women.

This bubbling acrimony came to the boil very quickly with a breach that was never healed. Soon after returning from Shrewsbury to Birmingham the word went round locally that the sisters could sing and they were invited on stage at the Metropole Theatre. Brother Teddy got to hear of this, went absolutely ballistic, and hurried to the theatre to order them home in disgrace.

Relationships were bad, and they got worse. Seventeen year old Dolly's boy friend, Edward Norton, was said to be a hard drinker, which made him not not dissimilar to the other young men, and so he wasn't popular with her mother and older brother, who seemed to see himself as her guardian after the death of her father.

On 25th July, 1910 Margaret, Florence Cunningham married the said Edward Norton, described as working in 'assembling'. The marriage certificate gives her age as 21. She was actually 17. Her birth certificate shows that she was born on June 5th 1893. "I was never able to do much schooling," she told us more than once in later life, hinting that helping her mother look after the house and menfolk was considered more important than getting educated. She possibly added a few years to her age so that she could escape.

To her, with what could have been a life of drudgery, marriage would have seemed an attractive escape. But if stability was what she yearned for, it didn't last long. Within the Catholic way of things at that time she had three children in double quick time, and then all all hell broke loose in the shape of World War 1. Her young husband and her two brothers went off across the channel to fight for 'King and Country' in the muddy maelstrom that constituted the unspeakable misery of trench warfare, and all that went with it. And they didn't come back.

So if Dolly had got married to improve her lifestyle then it didn't work. In harsh reality, destiny dictated the reverse. She was left as a young widow who was four years younger than the age recorded on her marriage certificate, virtually destitute and with three young children to rear in desperately difficult times.

She must have been in unimaginable depths of despair when an army mate of her late husband, who had been with him in the trenches, named Jack Potter, called on her to return his belongings. Edward Norton's worldly goods were in a tobacco tin, a cigarette lighter and not much else. A young husband went to war. A tobacco tin came back.

Fast forward some 20 years or so and Dolly Norton, now Our Mom, happily re-married to Frank Simms Shaw must have had a version of that heart-wrenching scenario rolling through her mind as the significance of the Prime Minister's message struck home.

By now she had ten children to worry about from, as I

believed, just the three marriages (hers and my dad's first marriage followed by the one to each other). Her second husband Frank had three daughters with his first wife, (who died very young), namely Mabel, Floss and Beattie and then there were mom's children - Teddy, Florry, Ivy and Jimmy. Frank, Tony and myself, the trio that mom and dad had together, completed our family.

Even Dolly and Frank's union was quickly marked by heartache when their first-born, known as 'Little Bertie', arrived on the scene prematurely. Our mother told us that poor Little Bertie was so small when he was born before his time that he could have been bedded down with clothing in a shoe box. Bertie didn't last long. He died within a day or two..

Now, a couple of decades on, she had good cause to be sick with fear as world War 2 broke out. Jim was call-up age and would certainly be in uniform before long and fighting somewhere or other not too long after that. Frank would be not too far behind. Please, God...no more 'tobacco tins'. Dad was too old to fight. Teddy was too old for the earliest conscriptions and, anyway, could be exempt because of being engaged in essential factory work.

Tony and I were far too young but this latest conflict had a terrifying new dimension compared to 1914-18. This time the Germans would drop bombs on us. Everyone on what was called the Home Front, in other words remaining in the UK, was at risk this time, and especially those who like us lived in the big cities close to industrial areas.

Bluntly, we were all actually living in a war zone. Bombs don't differentiate between adults, children and babies or the old and infirm. They kill or maim anyone and everyone in their path. To ease parents' concerns just a shade the government had introduced a programme of Evacuation, whereby, us kids could be sent off, with others from the same school, to countryside areas where the danger of bombing was considerably less.

Tony and I were to be evacuees, not once, but twice.

Chapter 2
'some enemy aircraft will inevitably get through'

The crocodile of kids stretched from the entrance to Small Heath railway station, along Golden Hillock Road, past the entrance to Armoury Road, over the canal bridge and down what we called 'the BSA hill.'

We had name tags pinned on us my big brother and I. TONY SHAW'. (known to me as 'Our kid, Senseless Tin Ribs, aged 9). And DENNIS SHAW (known to Tony as 'Our nipper, Fatty Brainless, aged six).

In the early days after the outbreak of war our parents twice accepted the opportunity to have us evacuated to the countryside, though the unfortunate timing of our fairly short excursions to first Worcester and then Gloucestershire meant that we were still in Birmingham for some of the worst of the bombing.

Throughout our frighteningly exposed and lonely little island all mums and dads were scared silly for themselves and almost frantic with worry over their children's future, or lack of it. So, for we youngsters, evacuation away from the towns and cities that were most at risk was considered to be a solution.

The first official opportunity for parents to have their children evacuated to the country had been issued by the Lord Privy Seal's Office in July 1939. It explained that while all was being done to prevent air attacks 'some enemy aircraft will inevitably get through' and therefore plans were being put in place to make the option available to up the three million children.

As soon as possible parents would be told where their children would be going. In many cases they were not told until some days after they had been taken. Mass evacuation to the country to live with total strangers for goodness knows how long began very soon after war was declared and was the immediate future of those of us in that particular queue and hundreds of others like it all over the country.

A gas mask in a red tin box with a strap was looped over our heads. In one hand we carried a small case of some sort containing what was to be our 'worldly goods' when we got to the selected 'safe destination'.

Even that short journey was feared to be hazardous. If there were to be a gas attack, in which the Germans unloaded a chemical killing cloud upon us, then we knew what to do. We had been shown how to don a gas mask just as diligently as we had been taught that ' 2 plus 2 are 4', or 'the cat sat on the mat', and instructions were on the inside of the box, just to remind us.

It was hardly a normal way to start one's education, but we knew about gas masks off by heart. Breathe heavily on the eyepiece and wipe it clean before putting it on. And better make haste if the gas has already arrived. Then:

1. Hold the Respirator by the straps.
2. Put on by first putting chin into the eyepiece and then draw the straps over the head. Adjust straps to obtain close but comfortable fit.
3. Take off by pulling the straps over the head from the back. (Do not take off by pulling the container up and over the face.)

If you ruined your gas mask by misuse you may not get another. Looking back, we didn't get told how to kick a football, how to hold a cricket bat or how to bowl a googly. There wouldn't have been much point. The former school sports fields by this time mostly housed either a barrage balloon or Royal Artillery guns.

Once fearful parents had placed their youngsters into the

charge of the teachers with their clip boards and lists they could only stand and watch, awaiting for the puff-puffing arrival of the locomotive-led train that would trundle the nation's future away to safety before the bombing began.

'Be good, won't you...Look after our Dennis...' Tony was told. At 9 years of age he had to grow up fast.

'Don't forget to wash behind your ears...'

'Write home straight away...'

'Don't cry. You'll be OK..' we were assured by mums who weren't too sure themselves.

Oddly, I've no recollection of being frightened, feeling hard done by, under-privileged or even unlucky. All I'd ever remembered was a blunt response of 'Stop moaning, don't you know there's a war on? ..' if ever I began to complain.

Our destination, Worcester, less than 30 miles from home, was pretty much off the anticipated Nazi bombing route but a couple of stray ones were to land there. On arrival that same crocodile of kids was shepherded forward, this time through the streets of Worcester and its outskirts, preceded by a teacher with two lists of names. On one, we refugees from the Blitz. On the other, local families who had volunteered to take in child. . 'One' mark you. Not two. Tony and I were two.

As the rest of the day wore on and dusk descended, the crocodile was reduced in length, not at all like Noah's Ark. His animals went in two by two. Ours went into their new, hopefully temporary homes, one by one. Twos were a different kettle of fish.

We ended up by the level crossing in Henwick Road in the district of St John's. There was a low wall and beyond it, in a small compact valley by the railway line, a country cottage surrounded by a little orchard as its garden. There the elderly lady, and her daughter agreed to take us in, two little lost souls needing a home away from the bombs.

We were led into a small sitting room with a dining table in the middle covered by a green tablecloth, an oil lamp sited in the centre. No gas or electrics. No inside loo.

Coal or log fire, I can't remember which. Most homes were cold in winter, other than near the fireplace. Central heating was for public or commercial buildings or the posh and the privileged. When folks like us were cold at home we just put on another layer of clothes, if you had any to put on.

We sat at the table, surrounded by scary shadows, and two total strangers, who were now our guardians, an elderly lady with wrinkled face and grey hair tied in a bun at the back, and a younger, comely one with a kind face and a nice smile. I can't remember any conversation in those awkward opening exchanges between total strangers of different age groups. Only the grandfather clock ticking away from the shadows.... tick...tock....tick...tock....

Soon the younger one removed the glass globe from the oil lamp and lit the wick, causing new shadows to dance around us as the flame flickered. That's all I can remember about the first night there, but then, next day, Tony and I explored the country garden with confidence coming back.

Life wasn't ALL bad. OK, we didn't know where our mom and dad were, but loved it at Henwick Road with its garden around the cottage, and pears on vines up the walls . Very popular we were, too, when we were allowed to give a few away to other evacuees after leaving afternoon school.

Soon we discovered, on that first trip, that life, as an evacuee had its benefits. Nobody had ill-treated us, we'd been given some nice food to eat, more plentiful in the country than in the big city we had just left, and there was fruit growing on those trees in the mini-orchard. Hostilities hadn't actually begun by then, remember, so there seemed to be an uneasy peace.

Best of all, on the nearby horse chestnut trees in the autumn there were conkers! (To the uninitiated a 'conker' is the large, shiny nut that grows inside the spiky green fruit of a horse chestnut tree. When the large green container falls and hits the ground, two or three conkers spill out of each one)

So how brilliant was that? Collect them when they fall, or throw up a stick to detach them from the branches. They were more highly polished than the most expensive furniture. You didn't see many of those little beauties in the inner ring of Birmingham, that's for sure.

If I remember anything clearly about being an evacuee in Worcester it was having a conker on a string and challenging other lads to a match. 'Mine's a conker 4' you would boast meaning that you had cracked open four other lads' conkers by means of well-aimed swipes with yours.

Then if your opponent had a new one on a string, a 'conker none', and he smashed yours his became a 'conker 5'. Great sport, but in later years, I discovered skulduggery went on. You could experiment in producing a champion conker by getting rid of the outer cover, soaking the kernel in vinegar and then roasting it the oven. The most important strategy, though, was to be able to pierce a clean hole in the centre, through which your string was threaded, without causing the start of a crack.

Throughout the remainder of my life I've experienced a little buzz of excitement whenever I've seen those lovely horse chestnuts gleaming on the ground. Oh to be a kid again for an hour or so. Just to play conkers. There's nothing a computer does to compare with it.

When we went down a little passageway to school, not far from Worcester Racecourse and the River Severn beyond, the local kids accepted us OK. If there had been any bullying, or resentment of the townies moving in I would have remembered. Anyway if any of the kids had tried to bully me they would have had Our Kid to contend with. Also, that elderly lady and her daughter proved to be a nice, kind, caring couple of temporary guardians that any two kids could have wished to be left with.

They probably quite liked having us if we behaved ourselves, and it wouldn't be too long 'cos Winston had told us all that the Germans hadn't a chance if we all 'did their bit' so they were joining in the war effort simply by looking after two young lads.

At home, however, our mom and dad found themselves in a dilemma. In those early months after the official outbreak of war not a lot had happened on the Home Front. It was a period that became known as The Phoney War. 'Perhaps it won't be too bad after all', the population began to think with unwarranted optimism but mom was pining, and worrying about our absence as much as she would have we been there so it was decided that members of our family, we can't remember which ones, were sent to take us home.

That strange, misleading period from September 1939 to April 1940, when despite the official outbreak of war there were no hostilities, much preparation went on. Barrage balloons were deployed to force enemy aircraft to fly higher than they would have liked, 400 million sandbags were created to pile around important buildings, shops and private dwellings and 38 million gas masks were distributed...yet there were no air raids.

So, as I recall, our evacuation to Worcester didn't save us from any bombs. But it was well worth the experience. I learned about conkers.

Chapter 3
"Wave after wave of Nazi bombers, some 350 in total droned over the city'

No longer 'evacuees' we were now back home again though at entirely the wrong time. Our return coincided with the end of the Phoney War that I mentioned in the earlier chapter.

We more or less arrived at the same time that the bombing of Birmingham began, a night-after-night offensive by the enemy designed to demolish factories and other selected targets, fracture railways and bury public morale under tons of wreckage.

Official figures released show that between August 1940 and April 1943, 2,241 citizens were killed and some 7,000 injured, many seriously. Some 2000 tons of bombs unleashed on England's second city demolished more than 300 factories and nearly 250 other buildings, many of them dwellings. In all it's reported that 5,129 high explosive bombs burst in Birmingham and 48 parachute mines. The number of incendiaries was beyond calculation.

In a more modern age of mass communication it is almost impossible to comprehend the fact that much of this was never reported at the time in order to avoid the possibility of mass panic. The country at large had little idea of what Birmingham and other main centres were going through.

Blitzing the heavily populated urban sprawl, with what later became know as collateral damage, was a very new kind of warfare. Apart from a clumsy flight by the infamous Zeppelin, and a misdirected inaccurate bomb or two, there had been no such strategy in the 1914/18 war with Germany simply because aviation technology had not advanced enough by then.

This new, lethal style of warfare had been first used

'effectively' only five years earlier in 1935 during the Spanish Civil War. To help General Franco subdue the factions contesting his Fascist regime, a sympathetic dictator, Adolf Hitler, orchestrated on his behalf the bombing of the Spanish town of Guernica when 15,000 innocent civilians were bombed out of existence.

The Guernica outrage was regarded as instrumental in Franco winning his campaign to put down all opposition from Republicans, Royalists and Communists. Now Hitler, having put it to the test with merciless results,was to use similar tactics against Britain and Tony and I returned from Worcester just in time for a taste of it. I've no way of recalling each air raid in turn, and nor has research helped me to marry up incidents with official dates. Advancing years have, inevitably caused all those many nights of Nazi aggression that we endured, and miraculously survived, to blur and converge more or less into one.

Real historians, those with factual data and a retentive mind to support them, must forgive me those passages that I intend to describe here in which a schoolboy's perspective and ageing memory fail to match up with dates in the record books.

Although, as I've said, memories of the various raids have blurred into one, the nightly routine became commonplace: the siren, the dash from warm bed to freezing cold, damp air raid shelter, the bombs, the fires, the fear, the false bravado and, at last, the all-clear. When it sounded to mark the conclusion of Germany's latest assault, a war-weary population of Birmingham would then start a new day, trying hard to pretend that it had all been just another minor inconvenience.

The marauding aircraft, having shed their weapons of mass disruption, distraction and destruction, were on their way back across the channel, the crews contemplating breakfast back home in Germany, a pat on the back to go with it, maybe, for a particularly nasty night's work well done.

We could only imagine the de-briefing." How much havoc did you create, Fritz? How many men, women and children did you kill or maim.? A hundred or two? Great stuff! Hitler and Goering will be delighted. Well done...have another sausage."

Down on the ground, there was no such sense of triumph, only relief that we were all still alive. Along with the weary neighbours we got to our feet to head for a few snatched hours in bed. Except that Our Kid and I had other ideas. Shrapnel. After such a night there would be treasures lining the roadways in the shape of jagged lumps of metal from exploded shells and the like, all sorts of remnants that young lads like us couldn't resist.

Often a road could be like a mouth with one front tooth missing where a house had received a direct hit and crumbled to the floor, all the bric-a-brac of normal life mixed with the rubble. Bedroom floor dipping crazily but still attached to one joist...bed deposited where the living room used to be on the ground floor, a teddy bear, a pillow, quite nice wallpaper.... perhaps a chamber pot.

Official records show that one such hideous raid went on for nine hours. Wave after wave of Nazi bombers, some 350 in total, had droned over the city, shedding a total of 400 tons of high explosive and 30,000 incendiary bombs on dear old, inoffensive Brum, leaving lives and property shattered, though not its spirit of defiance. As dawn was breaking after one of the raids, Tony and I did our usual runner from the air raid shelter in the direction of Fallows Road, on the far side of Walford Road, from where a glow in the sky signaled the certainty of a fire and fire fighters in action.

There, we stood transfixed as we viewed the inferno that

hours early had been the Queen's Gravy Salt factory, a short distance from the BSA. Firemen were directing their hoses at it, small groups of people, flames reflecting from their disbelieving eyes, staring at their personal vision of hellfire and wondering what really caused such madness.

All that we left was the remains of a few walls, some twisted iron girders and piles of rubble. Firemen were aiming their jets of water into the flames but in truth there was nothing left to save. This was one of the enemy's lesser achievements. OK, they robbed us of the gravy for our Sunday joint. But we didn't have a Sunday joint to put it on, anyway.

Amidst the mayhem, our married brother Ted's house in Victoria Road Small Heath was bombed to the ground...but he found, in a cupboard, alongside smashed glass and crockery, an egg unbroken. The house was virtually gone but a precious egg remained unbroken...so when he had found somewhere else to hang his hat, he fried it for breakfast.

In the kitchen our mom, as always, simply had to squeeze yet more energy and resolve from a body and mind that must have seemed drained of all senses. She'd been up all night, trapped in a tin shelter, distraught with fear for her family and herself, saying out loud 'Hail Mary' after 'Hail Mary' in prayer to her Roman Catholic God, wherever he might be. Now she had to get breakfast for two lads and herself before she went to work and they went to school, but they'd gone missing. Little devils....

Breakfast? Hardly any ration coupons left, very little money, shops with almost empty shelves, in the cupboard, by the old fashioned gas cooker, a tin of dried egg, a tin of spam and some not-very-fresh-bread. So, into the pan it went for a wartime version of bacon and eggs.

There can be no modern equivalent of Our Mom because she was the product of a unique age, a spell in world history that will never be repeated in the same form. When she died in September 1974 aged 81, a link was broken with two world wars, many years of grief and anxiety, a lifetime of pure simple honesty of purpose marked by the odd mistake, and the support of others in need, that later generations couldn't even attempt to copy.

She was still in the process of bringing up the last two of those ten kids from her two marriages, having sampled heartache, despair, poverty for a while, and lots of joy. You merely had to look at her hands, when in her mid and late years, to see the sort of life she had led. The palms were hard and calloused, the product of a thousand kitchen floors and front steps scrubbed, probably as many coal fires built and lit, and family washing pounded in a tub with a 'dolly" in what she called a 'maiding tub'...not to mention her spell on a factory lathe making war munitions.

In one classic Ma Shaw episode years later, in the 1950s, there was a severe coal shortage. When the only heating in your home, in the winter, is coal-fired, that's a major problem, though on a temporary basis at least, not an insoluble one as she demonstrated. For some strange reason (strange because nobody could play it) we had a piano at No.21. A jet-black upright one that took up space, but served no other purpose.

One early evening the sound of heavy banging could be heard emanating from the Shaw household followed by the splintering of wood. Inside the sitting room of the house, with its fireless grate, could be found our mother, unprepared to allow her family (probably only me left of it at home, by then) to be cold when they came home needing bit of warmth on a cold day.

She was swinging a coal hammer like a South Wales miner and pieces of piano were being flying off the frame to be then taken outside and smashed into smaller, burnable segments, for a fire to be lit so that her humble abode could be warm and welcoming to folks when they arrived home.

That was her in one scenario: "No coal for the fire? OK, I'll smash up the piano." She knew nothing of designer dresses, posh meals out, TV, motor cars, computers, mobile phones, texting, or foreign travel. She was simply 'Our Mom' to Tony myself and most of the rest of the family, 'Ma Shaw' to neighbours and in-laws, 'Mother' to my Dad, Frank, 'Aunt Doll' to nephews and nieces and 'Dolly' to her peers.

I don't recall ever hearing anyone call her Margaret, including Dad. He had called her Dolly, too, I gather before us kids heard him shouting upstairs to her and apparently we started copying him by calling her 'Dolly', as well so he switched to 'Mother'. Not very romantic, especially as he was older than her, but practical and it worked.

Our Dad, Frank Simms Shaw, was born on Christmas Day 1883, to John Shaw and Catherine Parker Shaw , formerly Heekes, ten years before mom. Because, as I've explained, mom and dad both had children from their previous marriage, a widow and widower merging their families together, and then adding three more, there were brothers and sisters, step brothers and sisters, and half brothers and sisters.

I've never believed in 'fate'. Events only seem to have been dictated by 'fate' after they have occurred. I'll never believe that anything that takes place was 'pre-destined' but if ever two people needed each other when they met it was mom and dad. In the early days of their courtship, ie. going out together prior to possible engagement and then marriage, mom lost another of her relatives.

Frank and Dolly went out for the day to New Brighton leaving mom's children with her mother, who then lived in Belgrave Road. By now mom was probably getting happy again but even that was brought to a momentary halt.

When she got back from New Brighton her mother was dead.

It seems my Grannie Cunningham, who died some ten years before I was born, had been sitting outside her front door in the yard, taking in some fresh air on a nice day, when a violent fight broke out between a group of young men. She became so agitated, perhaps shouting to them to stop, that she had a heart attack and died. It's true that mother and daughter had not always seen eye-to-eye, but she wouldn't have wanted her to go like that.

However, I've already described mom's heart-rending situation. Dad's was only moderately better.

His wife had died young leaving him living in a small house at 2 Summer Grove, Summer Road, not far from where mom lived, with three young daughters whom he could not hope to rear while also going to work to support them.

Against all his instincts he had to have them put into Birmingham City Council's care, though he had an elder brother, my uncle Bert, and a sister, Aunt Kitty. In those days of large families, poor health care, regular death of mothers in childbirth and high child mortality (i.e. death before the age of five), it was commonplace for families to take in children from other parts of the family who were in danger of being destitute.

For whatever reason dad's family didn't help him with his three kids and it was only when he met and married mom, on August 14th, 1920, that he could bring them out of care and the combined family started off by moving into dad's tiny homestead. All nine of them, that is, though it was soon to become twelve. At much the same time mom's sister, Ellen died in childbirth, leaving behind three children, so what did mom and dad do? They took them in and reared them until their father could make other arrangements. *"We've already got seven, what difference will another three make....?"*

To modern minds the thought of ten children of mixed parentage, and two adults, living in a small two-up-two-down with no bathroom and an outside lavatory across the yard, is beyond comprehension. Not then. With no other choice they just got on with it.

On Sundays the Shaw/Nortons would sit down to dinner, all twelve of them together, two parents, eight girls, two boys, squashed around one higgledy-piggledy table, and though it could have been the early ingredients of World War 2, those Sundays were in fact described by my half-sister Florry (known as Little Floss because there were two of them), as lovely, happy, often hilarious affairs. Makes you think, doesn't it....?

From that over-crowded beginning, and as children grew up to become wage earners, and some moving out to get married, far better times, and a period of comparative affluence arrived as the family moved to larger accommodation in Stechford, Coventry Road (where I was born) and the tree-lined Charles Road, Small Heath, when it was quite an upmarket location. Later, if anyone asked Tony and I to explain all the domestic equations we would trot out the cliché that 'we're all the same...just one big happy family, we're all brothers and sisters to each other', but it wasn't entirely true.

As I believe, from before I was born, or my memory began to take shape, along with the fun and the love, the parties and the day trips, there were likes and dislikes, petty jealousies, girlie petulance, blokey lack of consideration, too much of all that to pack into any one house and inevitably some moved out. By the time we moved to Ansell Road, around 1936, Mabel had married Harry Anderson, a Midland Counties amateur boxing champion, Ted had married Lilian while Florry was married to William Brown and Ivy was married to Syd...but that still left a family of eight to live in the corner terraced house in Sparkhill, with its two decent-sized bedrooms, one tiny one, and no bathroom or electricity.

Tony recalls, when aged five, walking with Mom and I to see 21 Ansell Road in 1936 and feeling very let down 'because all our previous houses seemed 'grand' in comparison. But the family had broken up with far less wages coming in and so, again we had to be packed into a much smaller dwelling. Mom and Dad slept in the main room, in which Tony and I slept head -to- toe in a single bed alongside theirs. Frank & Jim slept in the quite large second room and Big Floss & Beat somehow managed to sleep & share the 3rd bedroom, which subsequently became a bathroom and not a very large one at that.

We had gaslight with the small flames covered by a fragile little 'mantle, that virtually crumbled when you touched it. Heaven knows how many times Tony or I were sent running off down to one of the corner shops to buy another for about a half-penny before the light could go on. Bath night was a classic example of the times, too. Ours was not too dissimilar to those shown in film or TV drama of the miner coming home to his tiny miner's cottage and bathing in a tin tub in front of the fire, a strategically placed towel being the only defence of his dignity.

Our tin bath was kept hanging on a nail in the outside coal house where it collected coal dust and spiders while awaiting, for periods of at least a week, its next call to duty. Then it was dusted down and carried into the kitchen, placed between the sink and the brick-built boiler that had a space for a fire underneath. The boiler had to be filled up with bowls of cold water from the nearby tap to be heated by the fire beneath. In winter burning coals could be carried on a shovel from the living room fire to get it going. In summer the fire had to be lit with newspaper and one of the small bundles of firewood that little local shops always sold.

Once the water was heated sufficiently it had to be ladled from the fire into the bath...and then the order of usage was based on seniority or whatever mom decided so that meant Tony and I went in last. By then let's just say the water wasn't hot. And it wasn't all too clean either. Our sisters started to go the public baths at Sparkhill if they could afford the luxury and who could blame them? And so to bed. I've vague recollections of being covered by topcoats over the bedclothes in the coldest of weather, but the sleeping arrangements as a whole still didn't offer much privacy for the growing young women. Or young men for that matter.

I do recall that Floss and Beattie, now in their late teens or early twenties, went to live with Mabel and Harry in a back-to-back house, in Erasmus Road Sparkbrook and then Beattie married Thomas Caine, a boiler maker from Liverpool thereby reducing the inhabitants of No.21 to a more manageable six, namely mom, dad, Jim, Frank, Tony and I.

Beat and Tom went to live in a small back-to-back house in Lawden Road, Small Heath, not far from old house on Coventry Road by the old Kingston cinema and Birmingham City's St Andrews Football Club ground where I was born in 1933. Jim was a bakers' roundsman with the Co-op, or the Birmingham Co-operative Society to give its full name. Frank started off as a butcher's boy, found he couldn't stand all the blood and carcasses and moved on to become an apprentice toolmaker at the BSA. When the war began Jim was soon drafted into the army and the Worcestershire Regiment, stationed at Norton Barracks, Worcester, and Frank into the air force, based at RAF Wellesbourne Mountford, near Stratford-Upon-Avon.

That left Tony and I with mom and dad at a time when the whole world was in turmoil. Tony was nearly two and half years older than me and, boy, was I lucky to have him around when I needed him. Among the 10 was one of my many wartime heroes, Jim. After he joined the Worcestershire Regiment, Jim would come home briefly now and again and Tony and I were allowed to play with his tin helmet, rifle and backpack.

Jim led an extraordinary existence at that time, a lifestyle that, like his mother's, will probably never be repeated. Stationed as he was at Norton Barracks in Worcester his guard duties were not outside the main gates, but on top of the magnificent Cathedral, easily recognised as the majestic backdrop to so many lovely pictures and paintings of the New Road County Cricket ground.

From the top of the cathedral the enemy aircraft could be observed during their flight to bomb either Coventry or Birmingham or both, having flown across from Germany via France to the mouth of the Bristol Channel before following the route of the River Severn to Worcester from where they veered in an Easterly direction towards the more industrial West Midlands.

As a signaller his job was to report the volume of incoming flights to the authorities to at least give the artillery on the ground, the searchlight crews, the guardians of the barrage balloons and whatever other defensive strategists were on duty, some idea of what was in store as yet more aerial violence progressed deep into the night.

On other occasions, because he was the proud possessor of a small Hillman Minx motor car, he was back home in the heart of Birmingham with his family, sometimes having what was known as 'French leave', the practice of getting out of camp and back in again unnoticed and without permission.

"Sometimes I was watching from the cathedral as Birmingham was being set on fire or blown to bits," Jim has recalled. "On other occasions I was in the thick of it myself, by choice because I wanted to see how the family was coping." And there was another attraction back in Birmingham... Brenda George a local girl from Swanage Road Small Heath whom he married in 1941.

On one particular morning, after an all-night raid, mom would make sure a frugal breakfast would be ready, conjured from whatever happened to be available. But where are those two lads? They'll be the death of me. And we nearly were. As she arrived at the gate to shout us in from our shrapnel-hunting expedition, we walked round the corner of the street towards her.

I was carrying an armful of shrapnel. *Tony was carrying an unexploded incendiary bomb...*

Chapter 4
'...we could have been burned alive'

The incendiary bomb was an essential part of the enemy strategy in blitzing Birmingham and the other major cities and industrial areas in the UK. A nasty, lethal little object that caused fires, lit up a vicinity to help the bigger bombs to find their targets, it also heaped more fear on the local community

Chemicals such as magnesium, phosphorus or petroleum jelly (napalm) were used to explode into flames on contact with a building roof, a vehicle or the ground. The Luftwaffe tended to use thermite in eighteen-inch casings weighing only a couple of pounds. The average "breadbasket" was seventy-two incendiaries.

Deliberately, at a ratio of about one in ten, an incendiary bomb would be primed to hit the ground, bounce, and lie still, looking like a dud but still packed with its highly combustible filling, and ready to flare up with deadly, delayed -action, consequences. Which is why it really wasn't a good idea when at daybreak and the all-clear had sounded after one raid, our kid found one lying by a neighbour's doorstep...and picked it up. What happened in the next few seconds couldn't have been more dramatically stage-managed.

As we turned right out of Barrows Road into Ansell Road, alongside where we lived, our mother arrived at the front gate to tell us our breakfast was ready and we were to get ready for school. She was confronted by one of her sons carrying a bomb...

'Put it on the floor, carefully,' she snapped as Tony proudly held out the incendiary bomb, a souvenir that all the other shrapnel-seeking kids would envy. Or so we thought.

'But Mom...it's only a dud.' he started to protest. 'Put it on the floor. Carefully...' she repeated. When she spoke with that tone in her voice we didn't argue.

By then an air raid warden had moved in to smartly cover the bomb with sand from one of the obligatory buckets placed outside each house, alongside a bucket of water, as we were ushered clear of the German weapon of war. Then two Home Guard soldiers from Golden Hillock Road barracks at the bottom of Ansell Road were summoned. They took it to the nearby field and fired a bullet into it. The incendiary flared frighteningly and as it spewed out its deadly magnesium, burst into flames.

Tony's 'dud' was a live bomb. We both could have been burned alive as a walking firebomb.

Even for our mother, with all her wartime experience, this moment must have been a stomach-wrencher, though moments of potential panic were nothing new to her. Long before World War 2 broke out she had experienced more than any normal person's share, and then some....

There was that telegram dispatched by the War Office in 1915, the second year of World War 1, the message that had turned her from newlywed to widow in the space of a line or two of print. " Edward Norton has been killed in action." it read, or words to that effect. Tough luck. Edward had died for his country. Now Dolly could bring up his kids on her own.

He was just one of the wave after wave of young men, boys some of them, who went 'over the top from the trenches' into fields of mud and hails of shells and bullets fired by another group of young men on the other side. He was injured at the front and died in transit to a field hospital behind the lines.

Because of how the world was then, no one who knew him was able to visit his last resting place until about eighty years later when my brothers Tony and Jim found it, almost lost but not quite forgotten among all of the other lines of war graves.

When her young late husband's belongings were returned to her by another young soldier, one who had survived the enemy fire but had returned shell-shocked, probably, but still with a life ahead of him what was a young woman to do? Collapse in a flood of tears. Scream with hysteria. Or just get on with her life, looking after her young'uns best as she could.? Mom would have shed her tears in private away from the children, buried her grief deep inside, put on the bravest face possible, and carried on surviving the best she could.

Some time after that she met 'our dad', who must have been a rock of stability with his job in the Freight department of the old London, Midland and Scottish Railway. Her actual age was still only about 25/26 when they met and 27 when they married. She then became the mother or step-mother of a total of seven children that, due to her sister Ellen's death, was to become ten. No wonder that the Ma Shaw that I remember had matured in life to become as tough as old boots one moment and as kind and caring as a nun the next.

If one of the neighbours was having a baby and the midwife was late, send for Ma Shaw, she'll know what to do. If somebody's died, send for Ma Shaw. She had 'laid out' more than one dead body to lie with a degree of dignity until the undertaker arrived. Broken arm? Ma Shaw will put it into a sling so that you can catch the bus to the General Hospital. She loved a party, too. Get all the family friends and neighbours together, have a few drinks, a joint of meat and a few trimmings. All do your party piece, one by one, and everyone join in at the end:

"My old man, said follow the van....
"And don't dilly dally on the way...
"Off went the van with my home packed in it
"I followed on with my ol' cock linnet..."

After a few drinks the singing became really naughty, although us children never realised it at the time.

She'll be coming round the mountain when she comes
She'll be coming round the mountain when she comes
She'll be coming round the mountain, coming round the mountain, coming round the mountain she comes.
She'll be wearing Woolworth knickers when she comes
She'll be wearing Woolworth knickers when she comes

And so on, and so on, with innuendo following innuendo. While this was going on Tony and I, and our two pals of about the same age from over the road, Garth and Rex Salmoné, whose mother was always at our parties devised a great little party trick of our own. Until we got found out.

One of us, Tony probably, noticed that since the tablecloth swamped the table when the extending leaves were pushed back into place it provided a den underneath where we could all squat down unnoticed. We were injuns in our wigwam and it was strategically handy because many of the party goers would place their glass on the floor after each sip, whereupon we could sneak it under the table and pass it round. This rather exciting exercise meant that we could test the respective merits of M&B mild, All Bright bottled beer, port and lemon, sweet sherry and maybe a mouthful of rather foul-tasting bottled stout.

The ruse very quickly came to light when mom wondered what the kids were up to hiding under the table and I emerged drunk as a skunk, I can't remember at what age, but unable to stand up on legs that had turned to rubber. I learned about the danger of mixing your drinks at a very early age. Ma Shaw would always do her own party piece, too, no problem. *Black-Eyed Susan* One of dad's favourites, and she sang it with his bowler hat on her head, a walking stick in her hands, and a lovely soft smile in her cornflower-blue eyes...

I'm going back to the shack
Where the Black-Eyed Susans grow

Yet that caring, conscientious, sparsely-educated but capable lady could conjure up courage beyond the call of duty if any of her flock were threatened. I well recall a night when, early in the war years, brother Frank's wife-to-be, Winifred Woodcock, was assaulted. She and her family, had been forced by severe bomb damage to leave her home at the picture-framing shop next to Sparkhill Park on Stratford Road. She moved in with us while her parents, sister and brother made other arrangements.

Winnie's arrival was something of an eye-opener for Tony and I, our lesson No.1 in the lengths to which young woman will go in attempting to make the reflection that stares back at them from the mirror match their own high expectations. She took pride in her appearance, was always smart and well groomed. Her man might be away on RAF duty just now but standards weren't going to slip.

Every night before she went to bed she meticulously wound strip after strip of hair into a small metal device called a 'curler'. No matter what time it was, or whether the young men were blowing each other to bits around the world, seemingly dozens of curlers had to be carefully locked into place before a nylon scarf was tied over the top and it was time to seek some sleep.

Next morning the reverse ritual took place to the giggling, teasing amusement of Tony & I and the disbelieving frustration of poor old Ma Shaw who had more important problems on her plate than applying hair curlers by the dozen. True, Mom was sometimes known to shove in a couple herself, in order to have a curl or two at the front, peeping out beneath her own ever-present head scarf, but that took her about thirty seconds.

Winnie wasn't the only one, at that time, seeking refuge at the constantly-crowded Shaws. Our sister Beattie's husband, Tom, was sleeping on the floor downstairs awaiting the arrival of their daughter Margaret, in the nearby maternity hospital, to make us uncles again... Tony, aged not yet ten, and myself two and a half years younger. We already had a nephew in Ivy and Sid's son Roy and there were more to come, as it transpired.

Winnie worked nights in the canteen of the Joseph Lucas factory in Foreman's Road where the workforce toiled day and night on essential war work. Getting home was a disturbingly lonely business when she finished her catering duties entailing quite a lengthy walk when she got off the 'bus. This particular night was more disturbing than usual. There were footsteps behind her. Male footsteps.

No street lights shone to add a small glow of comfort. Every window of each terraced house was blacked out entirely by the obligatory thick curtains. To make it worse for her, and even more eerie, it was also a murky, foggy night. If she was lucky an Air Road Warden would be on patrol nearby. But not on this occasion when she needed one most.

Winnie hurried to get to the safety of 21 Ansell Road, unsure whether the footsteps were sinister or not. Mercifully, she was almost there when the stalker attacked her. Tony remembers vividly what happened next. Our family was sitting around, probably listening the news or Vera Lynn, and I was in bed, when suddenly there was a frantic banging on the front door and the sound of a woman screaming.

Mom dashed to open it and there was Winnie, virtually in hysterics, blood spattered on her face, clothing disheveled. Mom dashed past her daughter-in-law, into the street just in time to see the shadowy figure of a man duck into the passageway at the end of our garden some ten yards or so away.

After him she went, followed by Tony and the courage of all of his nine or ten years. The cowardly assailant was lying stretched out on the floor, presumably hoping to become invisible in the blackout conditions. As Tony recalls, mom grabbed him by the scruff of his neck as though he were a wayward dog, and dragged him back towards the house.

By then the red mist had dropped in front of her eyes, and no wonder. Things were bad enough in the thick of a war, without such scumbags attacking the wives or girl friends of the lads on the front line. He was lucky not to be lynched. The culprit had stalked our sister-in-law-to-be (or maybe they were already married, I can't remember) while she was walking home and had then tried to assault her..

As Tony recalls: "Mom started laying into to him so I followed suit, punching him as hard as I could. The commotion had attracted neighbours to come running out and when one said to mom 'Stop hitting him' she shouted back ' And you can shut up or you'll get one, too.' She was so incensed and upset at what had been done to Winnie, that she'd completely lost it.' "

Fortunately for the assailant, a would-be rapist presumably, two air raid wardens arrived to frog-march the culprit to the local nick leaving Ma Shaw to return to the house to soothe Winnie with the obligatory cup of tea.

For the Birmingham population, those years when Britain stood alone as Europe collapsed under the might of the German war machine, were a nightmare without end and all these years on it was woman like our mom who created and maintained 'the Dunkirk Spirit' as it was called while the men, mostly, actually fought the battles.

Scraping to put austerity meals on the table by day, rushing off to work to make munitions intended to kill fellow human beings, patching up clothing that should have been discarded as dusters, then shivering in a shelter shaken by exploding bombs by night. If there was just the sound of an explosion but no noticeable earth movement, then that particular bomb was a safe distance away. But when you heard the whistle of the in-rushing air through the fin of the missile followed by what felt like an earthquake nearby there would be a collective murmur of: "That one was close..."

A favourite muttered cliché among those huddled in their metal-covered hole in the ground was: "They say you never hear the one that gets you..." followed by a lengthy collective silence as the sufferers tried to work out whether that perceived wisdom was reassuring. Or not.

Sometimes for several hours the bombs exploded, the ack-ack guns fired shells into the night, the searchlights probed for the enemy raiders and the barrage balloons, floating around on the end of metal cables, were like flying sentries that probably did very little other than add to the clutter and the drama in the sky.

Down below our kid and I pondered the important questions that clog up boys' minds...were they *Junkers* bombers up above protected by *Messererschmitt* fighters?. Were there *Heinkels* with them or *Focke Wulfs*?. There could be *Stuka* dive bombers, too, circling like vultures, waiting to swoop down, a bomb aimer's finger on the button waiting for the BSA to arrive in his sight, too, but no matter.

Soon our *Spitfires* and *Hurricanes* would arrive, all piloted by real-life Biggles figures, and with a few well-directed rat-a-tat-tats of gunfire from holes in their wings to either shoot them down or send them back to Germany like the beaten rats that they really were going to become. Talking of rats, and beaten ones at that, there was Lord Haw-Haw.

Real name William Joyce, he was an American who was brought up in Ireland and had a strange, nasally and sneering transatlantic accent. A thoroughly disreputable individual, and serial turncoat, he was a Roman Catholic who informed on IRA rebels and became a senior member of the British Union of Fascists and fled England to Germany, changing his allegiance when he learned he was to be interned.

Fittingly, he became the last man hanged in Britain for treason in being the voice of Nazi propaganda throughout the war, transmitting from bases in Germany, to up to 16 million people in the UK. Known as 'Lord Haw-Haw', by a British population that possessed a disparaging talent to make fun of the most sinister opponents, he would use his broadcasts to portray us as cowering victims and the Germans, whom he'd changed sides to join, as the glorious victors in a crusade for world peace.

I recall clearly when my pal Alfred 'Bonny' Harvey, who lived adjacent to the BSA social club, where his father was steward, told me that this infamous traitor had said on one of his creepy 'Germany Calling...Germany Calling...' broadcasts (though with his sneering voice at came across the crackling airwaves as 'Jairmany Calling') the night before that the Luftwaffe had a 'silver bomb for Golden Hillock Road...'

Golden Hillock Road was where the Harvey family lived, just across the canal and sports field from the BSA factory that Hermann Goering and his bombers longed to send crashing to the floor to stop the manufacture of small arms and other ammunitions that could be used against them.

And joke though we made of him, such was Lord Haw-Haw's uncanny prophesies of which targets in Britain were next on the Luftwaffe's agenda of destruction, he obviously had access to accurate information, and certainly his reported reference to the well-bombed factory in Golden Hillock Road tended to bear it out.

Chapter Five

'...their world fell in on top of them, it was hell on earth.'

The silver bomb for Golden Hillock Road, said to have been mockingly predicted by the odious Lord Haw Haw, found its target on the night of November 19, 1940. The BSA factory, its machines humming with activity as the night shift workforce churned out more and more essential munitions, proved to be its bull's eye. The damage it caused was cataclysmic.

When it exploded the shock waves seemed to rattle the teeth of all those frightened folk huddled in shelters nearby. Everyone knew what had happened. "They've got the BSA..." was all that needed to be said, and for tortured souls who were directly beneath it, when their world fell in on top of them, it was hell on earth.

The air raid began in early evening, around 7.30 pm. Many inside the factory had been taken by the surprise as the sirens sounded only a couple of hours after the November nightfall, earlier than usual. Some of the workers hurried to the factory shelter as the bombs started to fall and the gunfire crackled overhead. Other remained behind, working away, listening to the radio, swapping jokes and ribald banter.

There had to be music, an accordion playing popular songs of the day, and the there had to be humour. Without these two ingredients the population of the UK would have caved in.

When the bomb found its target high on the building, the upper floors went crashing down in hundreds of tons of bricks, machinery from other floors and steel girders, crushing some 80 factory workers to death and burying many others alive underneath.

One man, a local worker who we'll call Fred, was trapped for nearly nine hours before he was rescued. The massive girder that had dropped on him had a bend in it. That bend curved over his body, pinning him down but sparing his life. What happened after the bomb fell, was a story of epic survival almost beyond belief, as Fred later recalled in graphic detail. He had been knocked cold by a blow on the head as the factory caved in on him. He had no idea for how long he was unconscious but he woke up to a scene that no human being should have to endure.

The remains of two of his workmates lay sickeningly misshapen beside him. Yet, to his astonishment and relief, he was not seriously injured himself, thanks to that miraculously shaped girder. One foot was trapped by tons of debris. Otherwise he was as well as any man could be when a factory has fallen on top of him. "I began to wonder if it was crushed," he recalled "and made frantic efforts to get it free. It must have taken best part of an hour so for I was hemmed in on all sides, and above my head, by machinery, concrete and brickwork...

"Having got my foot free, and finding it was only strained a little, I wriggled and twisted to a small space on the floor, that looked like an ordinary fireplace and about as large. How this small space came to be left clear near me, must have been the hand of providence," he added. Around him, trapped and terrified, men and women were screaming out in agony for help. Fred joined in the frantic chorus of hope by shouting his loudest to attract the attention of would-be rescuers. That's if there were any...

"What an escape, to be still alive," he thought. "But escape from what, I wonder? I am in a living tomb." Intense fear took hold of him, and he joined in the shouting again with those poor wounded and dying souls nearby though they had no idea of the depth of the ruins packed in a chaotic heap above them. Perhaps no one on the outside could hear their cries.

"Then a fire had started near my feet and was starting to burn furiously," Fred's nightmarish account continued. "This increased my fear. I sat there watching that fire, wondering how long it would be before everything around me would burn." The fire was now burning not only the wooden bench he was sitting on but the bodies of his two late workmates also. The smoke began to get down his throat. Then there's a trickle of water from above, and he realises that they are trying to put out fires above. "What shall I do? I think of Mary, and wonder what she will do when they tell her I am gone. I offer up prayers as hard as I can pray for both Mary and myself. My boot catches fire and I cannot get my legs back far enough from that fire to put it out.

"What's the use, I ask, shall I bang my head on something and let the fire see me off, at least I shall not feel it then. Other parts of my clothes catch fire and I become frantic in my efforts to put them out, for I have no room to turn about. Then I decided I must keep calm and use my head, for I notice the smoke from the fire is commencing to blow away from me, and the air gets a bit clearer. So I think that if I can keep under the machine the fire will keep burning away from me."

This calmed him a shade and he decided to have a smoke if he could. He still had his pipe in his pocket and, after a good deal of twisting he got to his tobacco and matches. "The tobacco was fairly dry, although by now he was himself soaked to the skin by the encouraging flow of water from above. Although he could fill his pipe his matches were sodden and that's where the threat of fire worked in his favour. "I had to hold two matches by a hot cinder until they flickered up and I managed to light my pipe," he wrote. "Ah! That was better. A bit of comfort..."

Water was now beginning to collect on the concrete floor on which he was half sitting, half lying, and he began to have thoughts of getting his death of cold, so he pulled loose pieces of concrete towards him and wriggled them underneath him to sit on, although water was now dripping off his trousers. "I began to shout again, 'help...help... help' but there was no response. I realised now that I must lie there and wait, but for how long? Could I keep my senses until someone got to me? Yes, I made my mind up I would, and so I reclined there thinking, thinking hundreds of things, mostly of my wife and home.

"Time drags on, so I start shouting again. After a while I fancy I can hear an answer to my cries. I become frantic now and shout still louder. I listen and can faintly hear someone answering me, but they sound miles away. After a while I make out they are asking me where I was before the crash. I shout out my position from the outside wall near the canal and I can hear them telling me to hang on. So my prayers are answered I think, I am in touch with outside.

"Then I can hear rumbling noises above me, and I realise they are moving wreckage to get at me. I wait. It seems hours. Why don't they hurry? Little did I know until afterwards the amount of debris they had to move. I was now excited and still kept shouting to them, and then I can hear them shouting down a small hole, almost over me. They ask me if I am injured or crushed, I tell them I am all right except for the fire.

"They drop a rope down and pull me up and up until my head is through the hole. Then by grabbing my arms I am dragged through the hole to freedom and never did it seem so sweet as this moment. I shook their hands and found myself crying with joy and I felt they were crying too."

Planes were still overhead, and bombs were dropping as they took him by ambulance, in a bad state, shaking all over from shock and exposure, to a medical station. " The doctor said I was to be taken to hospital, but I have enough life in me to tell him there was no hospital or nurse who could look after me better than my wife. I was going home."

When they arrived at Fred's home another trauma lay in wait. The house where he and Mary lived had been bombed, as he recalled. "Although my back was almost broken I jumped out of the ambulance and after a quick glance at broken windows and doors, I ran down the house shouting at the top of my voice. He got no answer so he fled to the back door, which was burst off its hinges, and shouted some more. **And there she was.**

She had been taken next door and hearing his cries came running round to him. "We clung to each other. We cried together, crying with joy and fear. As we clung together we could each tell that we had been through a terrible night. Two souls with a single thought, 'thank God you are safe'. The fire was lit and Mary dressed him in warm clothes, attended to his cuts and burns, quite forgetting her own feelings from her ordeal.

"What a nurse, what a spirit, a true Briton with true English pluck. I thank her for all she did for me. We then sat down and told each other our experiences of the night, and with tears of joy and thankfulness we thanked God for sparing us to each other. So ended a night we shall never forget, and to anyone who reads this little story I would say: "Never give up hope, you die of despair"

First chance we got, not long afterwards, Tony and I made our way along the canal towpath to get as near as we could to what was left of that part of the BSA, and stood gazing at an area where, as all the locals knew, people had been buried alive. "There are dead bodies under the concrete slab," he told me, a child unable to grasp the severity of it all. "I know" I shrugged, equally detached at this tender age from the reality of mass murder under the heading of 'World War 2'.

Note: The above, with actual names changed, is a version of an incredible true story, deeply moving and very well presented, on the website WW2 PEOPLE'S WAR, written by the public and gathered by the BBC. (www.**bbc.co.uk/ ww2people**swar)

Chapter 6
'...No designer stubble for Frank Simms Shaw'

Our Dad was a kind of Mr Pickwick figure, and just as loveable. Meeting and marrying him was probably the best thing that happened to Mom in her entire life. In the period before my personal memory clicked into place, and before tensions set in as members of the mixed family became teenagers, the Shaw-Norton enjoyed what sounds like a happy family life.

I can't remember much about those very early days of my life but one of the things I remember mostly about Dad was his 'going to work routine', each afternoon for yet another shift that took him into the early hours of the morning. It began, in the tiny kitchen with the daily shaving ritual.

Boil a kettle of water on the old gas cooker. Pour it into a mug. Dip the shaving brush into water, rub the brush vigorously on the top of a small cylinder-shaped piece of shaving soap and lather up his chin and upper lip before carefully, strip by strip, removing his whiskers with a small razor containing a double-edged blade.

This meticulous procedure was repeated for a second time to ensure that not one whisker, or part of a whisker, remained. No designer stubble for Frank Simms Shaw, 'one of the old school' if ever there was. I don't recall him wearing anything other that a three-piece suit for work, waistcoat buttoned over braces that kept his neatly-pressed trousers up, white detachable collar freshly starched each day, affixed by collar studs, front and back and with the obligatory necktie, a Tootal no doubt, neatly tied.

His hair was of the purest white, not grey, but white... and had been, we were told, since he was in his twenties. On his feet were smart, light lace up boots, with a shiny toecap, brushed and polished each time before use.

By then mom had prepared his small attaché case complete with packet of sandwiches to eat during his nocturnal break, each slice of bread as thin as it was possible to cut with the sharpest of knives and covered with butter, or maybe it was margarine, right into each corner. No 'doorstep' slices for our dad, and not even the merest of areas on any slice unbuttered.

"Frank's very particular..." mom would tell neighbours with pride at the attention she had to pay to sending her husband off to his duties as a 'white collar worker' in area where mostly the menfolk worked in factories or on the buses unless they were up of 'call-up' age. In that case they were in uniform.

"Your father's got a wonderful memory," she would tell us. "There isn't a railway station in this country that he doesn't know. If any of the other clerks don't know they ask your dad. He always knows. They keep on asking him to be the boss of the department but he doesn't want the responsibility."

The 'class' system of the day deemed that manual workers were categorised as 'blue collars' and non-manual workers were 'white'. To meet this criterion Dad, conventional to the last, had his dress standards to uphold, though that's where the 'snobbery' seemed to end.

The last things he did before setting off on his walk to the bus stop en route into town, and his workplace in Suffolk Street goods department, were to clean his spectacles with the bottom of one of the curtains and and then to brush his bowler hat so that every speck of dust, real or imagined, was removed. Now he was ready to be seen in public. I don't ever remember him going out dressed any other way, apart from on holiday at Blackpool in 1939 when war was about to break out.

Once we were on the beach, deck chair at the ready, he would take off the collar from the studs, remove his waistcoat so that his braces were on show and, if the sun were threatening to burn white skin, place a handkerchief knotted at each corner on his head. When 'paddle time' arrived he would roll up his trouser leg to just below the knee and join in the fun at the waterline with us kids and mom, who lifted her dress to just above the knee. No higher. Not ladylike.

All of that might make him sound like something of a cold fish or fuddy-duddy, which he certainly was not. He loved to laugh and said that the nicest sound in all the world was a baby chuckling when you tickled its tummy. He would talk to everybody's kids 'even some runny-nosed ones in a pram' mom once said.

Along with a majority of his generation, Dad adored Vera Lynn and the messages of hope she wrapped up in the songs that she selected to sing in a simple, pure voice with perfect diction, all delivered with an honesty and sincerity that's impossible to adequately describe. Every word of her songs had a meaning, and you could hear each one of them clear as a bell, and with no gimmicks nor false transatlantic accent.

Future generations perhaps found it all rather corny, but then their loved ones hadn't been torn away to fight, and maybe to die, in the most horrendous circumstances imaginable.

There'll be bluebirds over,
The white cliffs of Dover,
Tomorrow, just you wait and see.
There'll be love and laughter,
And peace ever after....
Then, perhaps, came
We'll meet again.
Don't know where,
Don't know when
But I know we'll meet again
Some sunny day.

Simple sentiments, simply sung, yet when Dame Vera reached her 90th birthday some seventy years later, and sang them again, her record went to the top of the charts again, so she was right wasn't she ?

Dad's favourite meal was sharp cheese and crusty bread with a slice of Spanish onion and half-a-pint of M&B mild, partaken in the grounds of a local pub with Tony and I playing at cowboys and indians nearby.

"That's a mighty fine six-shooter ya got there, Hank..!' our kid would say to me, with the best imitation he could muster of Buck Jones on screen at the Olympia, the local Saturday morning fleapit cinema in Ladypool Road as I stuck out the first two fingers of my left hand and clenched the other three to look like a pistol.

"You gorra purty good gun yourself, Hank..." I'd drawl with top lip drawn back in a cowboy-like snarl as he aimed his seven-year old fingers back at me. 'Gunfight at the OK Coral' it was not. In our little minds far more blood thirsty than that....

Mom's other 'big treat' after going out with dad for two or three half-pints of mild to the local (he never drank bitter, and never had pints) they might go to the nearby fish and chip shop." We don't walk along the street eating out of the paper," she would say proudly. "We sit at a table and eat it in the shop on a plate, and with a knife and fork." How posh was THAT...?

Sometimes, before the outbreak of war, we would catch the No.8 Inner Circle bus from Walford Road to Coventry Road and change to a trolley bus, run by overhead electrical cables, the power transferred to the vehicle's motor by an arm attached to its roof. That took us to the city boundary at Sheldon from where we would stroll to a little country pub called the The Cock, at Elmdon, on the edge of Chelmsley bluebell woods, many years before it became a huge housing estate.

We would get a glass of lemonade each and a packet of Smith's crisps with a little blue bag in salt waiting to be scattered onto the contents. Then came the big, big treat in the shape of a further stroll along the Coventry Road to Elmdon airport where, if we were lucky, we might see a propeller-driven aeroplane take off or land.

The only 'day out' to surpass the magic of that little outing was to travel on the tram to the Lickey Hills with, to us, their mountains, forests and valleys where we could pretend to be Canadian Mounted Police, clicking our tongue to imitate the sound of galloping hooves. Fast forward 20 years or so from that date and, on the very same slopes I was reprimanded by a uniformed park keeper who came across me in a loving embrace with the lovely young woman who was to become my wife.

Better than cowboys and indians, I was to discover.

"That's a *fine* exhibition in a public place..." he declared, clearly affronted or embarrassed, or both, by our ardour, as we scrambled to our feet brushing away the leaves from our clothes, and me the lipstick from my face. And we were only kissing, for heaven's sake. Honest...

However, I digress: Dad's favourite sport was cricket and he reckoned, when he was younger, he could bowl a 'googly'. Howzat for skill! We believed him , of course. He was our dad...He recounted tales of his cricketing heroes playing at Edgbaston, including JWHT Douglas who was something of snail when it came to scoring runs. 'We used to say his initials stood for Johnny-Won't-Hit-To-Day,' he told us.

Next to cricket he loved football, and Aston Villa in particular. Pongo Waring's feast of goals...Eric Houghton's thunderous shooting and unstoppable penalties...the club's legendary half-back line of the 1930s...Gibson, Talbot and Tate. "They're more famous than Freeman-Hardy-Willis," he told us. At that time us kids hadn't the faintest idea that in a foreign land a weird little man with a black moustache the size of a couple of postage stamps smudged onto his upper lip, wanted to blow us to bits or burn us to a cinder.

Mercifully, because of how his age fell, Dad wasn't called up to fight in either of the two world wars and that was assuredly a blessing. Mom had lost one husband to German gunfire. Frank Shaw had found her when she most needed an honourable, unmarried man in her life.

This was the gentle gentleman who came home from work one morning after a particularly evil blitz. Yet, having done so, he was moved to return before going to bed, as he normally would. Instead he took Tony and I back into the city centre with him to see what damage had been wrought to the office block that he and his colleagues had been forced to vacate a few hours earlier, during yet another night of senseless killing and mayhem.

We heard him telling mom about how the office caught on fire while he was on his hands and knees sheltering under his desk. "My head was freezing and my backside was burning," he said, his sense of humour still intact despite the horrors of a night when innocent, decent ordinary men and women were blitzed out of their workplace.

He stood in Navigation Street, holding Tony with one hand and me with the other, looking at the blackened skeleton that used to be where he worked. Spirals of smoke were everywhere. It was a scene of massive destruction and smoke-filled misery as fireman poured gallons of water into what was left of Suffolk Street goods offices.

I heard a small sound above my head and looked up. It was the first time I realised that dads could cry.

Seeing his place of work smashed to the ground and left as a smouldering ruin moved him deeply but very soon afterwards the freight office had been re-established at the goods yard at Camp Hill and the railways continued to operate. This capacity of the working population to just get on with the job and ignore, so far as was possible, the inconvenience of the German war machine depositing plane-loads of bombs on top of them, was exemplified by thousands of folk back home who, in their own way, were as heroic as the men and woman on the front line.

One of these was George Taylor, a locomotive driver on the Great Western Railway who, like our own father was too young for WW1 and too old, or too important in the job that they did towards the war effort on the Home Front, for the WW2.

George, his wife Floss and four children Stan, Eileen, Audrey and Jean, had moved just before the war from a tiny cramped house by the railway line in Duddeston, a mile from the centre of Birmingham, to a modern semi-detached at 104 Hodge Hill Road, Ward End, thereby upgrading their lifestyle as few in those surroundings ever did.

George was the traditional kind of working man, a wage earner who provided a weekly sum for housekeeping but, apart from keeping the garden ship-shape contributed little else to the running of the house while expecting a meal to be on the table whenever he needed it. Floss was a rather shy, undemanding and lovable lady who, remarkably, made the housekeeping go around well enough to methodically save the deposit on that new semi-detached house to which the family moved in the mid-1930s.

Only later did the extent of that visionary move become clear. Who knows what their future would have been had they remained living near the railway sidings. Now her family were able to set their sights higher in terms of what they did with their adult lives, Audrey for instance being sent to a fee-paying Secretarial College because of her obvious brightness at junior school.

Yet, although situated on Birmingham's outer ring and away from the most heavily bombed areas of the City, the Taylor's house was not out of harm's way by any means. Measured as the crow flies, for instance, the famous Fort Dunlop, later to become an iconic building just off the M6, was only two miles or so away. Tyres of all description for a whole range of military vehicles were produced at the Dunlop while, in 1938, the Air Ministry had bought a site nearby, next to Castle Bromwich Aerodrome, where a factory was set up to produce the famous Supermarine Spitfire.

This was the legendary fighter plane that, when added to the Hurricane, was to defeat the might of Germany's Luftwaffe in the Battle of Britain. Massive damage could have been inflicted on Britain's defences, and means of attack, if direct hits had landed in that vicinity. Night after Night the Hun tried. They really tried....and from time to time, this meant that stray bombs would sometimes find their way to the Hodge Hill Road area. But mercifully the Luftwaffe's efforts to inflict serious industrial damage to help their wicked war aims failed miserably.

As their bombs spread death and destruction around the general public in Erdington and its surrounds, the Castle Bromwich Aircraft Factory, like Fort Dunlop, survived to do its job magnificently, producing fighters that were to pursue the marauding enemy and shoot them out of the skies. By the time the Castle Bromwich Factory closed in 1945,(at the time of writing owned by Jaguar Cars), a total of 12,129 Spitfires had be been built there by its wonderful workforce of local Birmingham men and women.

Fast forward fifty years or so and millions of motor cars a year encircle what is known as Spitfire Island, adjacent to those Jaguar Works. Situated there is a huge ironwork Sentinel Spitfire sculpture, designed by Tim Tolkien, grandson of Birmingham author, J.R.Tolkien. How many of the drivers, one wonders, realise the violent events that led to its construction ?

One example of the attempts the Germans made to hit specific targets in the Dunlop area was when a lone enemy bomber made it through the UK defences in broad daylight without a siren being sounded. Audrey and her father happened to notice an aircraft it in the sky in the Erdington/ Castle Bromwich direction and assumed it was one of ours.... until it released a bomb and they were able to watch until it disappeared from sight. They never found out what damage it caused. Just one more explosive device to add to Birmingham's misery.

On one of the family's nights of sheltering in their air raid shelter there was a huge explosion when a bomb landed in a garden a few doors away, demolishing a neighbour's shelter. Happily it was empty at the time, so no one was killed. However, the deep crater that it inflicted, became a play area for the local children, who would use one of the curved lengths of corrugated iron Anderson shelter walls, as a large toboggan.

My wife (of some 54 years as I write) still has a slightly crooked front tooth to prove it, sustained when the impromptu slide pulled up suddenly... but her face carried on.

Her dad, George, was born in Burton-on-Trent, home of some of the UK's finest breweries whose products played an important role in the life of a population for whom a beer and a debate about everything from football to politics via sex and the favourite in the 2.30 at Newmarket, were a buffer between too much work, too little money and a life that would otherwise have been drab and uneventful.

While George was a character known by pretty much everyone who either travelled on the same as bus as him or drank in The Raven pub a couple of hundred yards or so from his home, Floss was more of an introvert. Her children were her life.

George had originally worked as a teenager in a brewery in Burton, married Floss Barton who, as a young woman did some dancing on the stage, moved to Birmingham and became a fireman on the railway before progressing to become an engine driver, a job that hundreds of thousands of lads aspired to in their early years. That includes yours truly, by the way.

To be actually in charge of one of those coal-fired, steam-driven and majestic monsters that inspired awe and fear in equal measure as they charged along the track effortlessly pulling lines of either passenger coaches or rattling freight wagons must have sent a sense of power coursing through the very veins of the driver.

As I understand it George Taylor had driven them all, from the hurtling expresses to the gentle puff-puff local stopping trains, first as a fireman, stripped to waist in the fierce heat of the cab on warm days, feeding the ever open mouth of the flaming furnace with shovel after shovelful of coal, and as a driver, his one hand permanently bent to perfectly fit the dead-man's handle.

When the war arrived the railway service doubled and trebled in importance to the nation. There was military personnel moving around incessantly, snatching a short break at home, maybe, before heading for the trenches and all manner of essential goods to be shifted around. Few people had cars in those days and rail travel was comparatively inexpensive.

Against that background the engine drivers and their trusty fireman, went out on their journeys in the full knowledge that they could be a juicy target for enemy aircraft, especially when daylight raids were undertaken. It was not unknown for trains to be machine-gunned by diving German fighters in broad daylight. George appears to have had a simple attitude to the ever-present danger of being bombed. He ignored it, did his job, then went for a beer. Or three.

His children recalled afterwards how, if he was at home when an air raid began, they went down the Anderson shelter that they had joined together to install in the garden. He simply went to bed, and to heck with the enemy planes, but with one understanding. Since he had already had a long day at work, followed by a trip to The Raven before supper, someone had to wake him up so that he would be on good time for his next shift.

As there were no all-night buses then and Saltley Railway Sheds were six or seven miles away, it meant a long cycle ride to work before chuffing-chuffing off in his newly-fired-up locomotive, on yet another journey, possibly in the thick of a blitz. To ensure that he wouldn't be late the oldest child in the shelter, which was Eileen, had to scuttle up the garden path, ignore the menace that could be threatening from the skies, run upstairs and wake her dad, and then run back to the shelter.

By this time Stan was in the Royal Navy doing his bit for the nation somewhere on the high seas, having during his teenage years helped the war effort by acting as a messenger for air raid wardens police and emergency services on his trusty pedal cycle. His young sister, Audrey remembers it all clearly now, 70 years on, just as I recall how it was for Tony and I, some 10 miles away across the other side of the city as the crow flies.

She was, of course, the young lady with whom I was canoodling on the Lickey Hills some 10 or 12 years later when the park keeper was so affronted by our public display of affection. He wasn't to know that the feelings were going to last, at the time of writing, some 58 years including a Golden Wedding celebration.

Considering all of the preparation and planning that went into children's education later, after the war, it seems something of a miracle that we blitz kids managed to carry on with ours. This, mark you, despite, in the case of Tony and I, goodness how many nights in an air raid shelter followed by an hour or two snooze on the assembly hall floor before lessons, and two periods of displacement to small village schools.

Heavily in our favour, maybe, was the attitude to elementary education in those supposedly less sophisticated times. We were taught the alphabet and how to count to a hundred very early on. We chanted out the 'times tables' endlessly collectively, as a class, until we knew what, say, eleven elevens were without stopping to think. Spelling mistakes were frowned on, correct grammar and punctuation were essential basics and so by the time were about ten we could read, write and add up. What's more if we misbehaved, or were cheeky to adults we were punished and sometimes smacked. Sounds simple enough, don't you think?

In the thick of all this, incredibly, our parents put our names forward for for the entrance exam to the fee-paying King Edwards V1 Grammar School for Boys, Camp Hill, while the war was still on, Tony in 1941 and myself in 1943, and we both passed. Not many kids in the area where we lived went to Grammar School but we were the lucky ones. It shaped the rest of our lives and kept us out of working in one of the local factories.

It also introduced us to a standard of discipline that we would never otherwise have known. The teachers were unmistakeable because of the the black cloaks they wore. Two examples of the punishment you could receive are still burned into my brain, or rather one onto the side of my face and the other into my buttocks.

One morning I was a shade late for lining up in 9 a.m assembly and, in trying to catch up with classmates ahead of me, further along the corridor, I ran straight into one of the teachers 'Bill' Drysedale who was standing near the entrance to the hall with a hymn book in his hand.

"What's the hurry boy..." he bellowed, grabbing my by the throat. "I'm trying to catch my friends, sir..." I gulped. "We don't run to assembly, boy," he said quietly this time. "We walk..." and he smacked me firmly across the face with the hymn book. I never ran to assembly again, but the episode was something of a contradiction when you think about it. Us kids were being taught to sing hymns of love and peace from the book but the teacher slapped me across the face with his copy....

Around the same time, when at the school sports ground, ready to play rugby, one of the lads pointed out the rosy red apples in one of rear gardens adjacent to the field at the back of the pavilion, out of sight of the sports masters, or so I thought. Something of a show-off in those days, ready to take on most physical challenges, for lads my age, I was sitting astride the lowest bough of the tree in next to no time, tossing apples over the fence to the line of lads that had gathered to join the fun. Unluckily for me, the disturbance it created attracted the attention of our head sports teacher, Taffy Davies.

'Report to the pavilion steps...', he ordered me, '...bend over and touch the third one with both hands.' In this position, wearing only my thin rugby knicks, as we called them, on my bottom half, he gave me three swipes across the backside with a length of hosepipe as all the other boys stood in a semi-circle watching. I've never scrumped apples since. Nor did I feel I was the victim of unnecessary violence, or blame either Bill Dryesdale or Taffy Davies for teaching me how to behave.

Chapter 7

'...a fiery halo above...it would have been beautiful had it not been so deadly.'

One night of violent mayhem in particular sticks in my memory so vividly to this day that I can replay it like a mind's eye video clip that gives a flavour of what it was like to be at the heart of the infamous Birmingham blitz and may have been the 'final straw' that convinced mom and dad that we had to be evacuated again.

Incendiary bombs are bouncing off the rooves opposite, causing small fires on the pavements and roadways below... shadowy silhouettes in ten helmets are emerging from the darkness, risking serious injury or death to put them out on behalf of us all..Above them searchlights probe the dark sky. Up there somewhere are German aircraft ready to rain down more of their silver, cylindrical, little fire bombs at us. They could cremate all of us alive...

Watching them from comparative safety, but only a few yards away, are Mom,Tony and I, and a few neighbours as each amateur firefighter points a stream of water at the flames and another ordinary citizen behind pumps away at the gallon or so of water in a fire bucket.

Backlit by the flickering golden glow of the incendiary bomb fires, these are our neighbours, the wartime ARP (Air Raid Protection) wardens in the heat of their duties. Not quite the Home Guard of the TV classic 'Dad's Army', but a slightly older version of Joe Public battling throughout the night to keep us safe as Hitler's air force rained bombs on us. Barrows Road was a remarkable sight. Fierce fires dotted at intervals in the roadway, groups of firefighters visiting them in turn to put them out, all of it with a fiery halo above that would have been beautiful had it not been so deadly.

Four or five of us had been herded into the entry between the terraced houses and ordered to lie face down for our own safety. We were sheltering there, not far from our home, because of twice earlier being robbed of the comparative comfort of an Anderson Shelter. Instead of lying there on the cold, hard floor we should have been gathered in our own shelter. Comprising curved corrugated iron sheets, bolted together at one end to make a u-shaped cover, and fitted into a large hole dug in the garden, then covered with soil for added resistance against impact from above, most households had one.

No one inside would have had a snowball in hell's chance if a bomb scored a direct hit, as some did, but a useful shield against blast, and better than being inside a building when one of Hitler's bomb arrived. That particular night our own shelter was uninhabitable because rain had seeped in to it, leaving it calf deep in cold water.

So when that chilling drone of the air raid siren wailed after nightfall, we and some neighbours were hurried to a shelter in the garden of the house opposite where the family, and the one next door - the Stantons if I remember correctly - - had moved temporarily to stay with friends or family in the country and thereby escape the blitz.

These tiny, half under-ground salmon tin-like 'dwellings', measuring a few feet approximately square, were usually desperately cold in the the thick of winter. Only a small oil lamp was allowed for 'heat' and 'light' but this one quickly became airless and stuffy with several people huddled in it. And that wasn't all...

One of the menfolk put his hand against the left side corrugated iron. Then against the other. Unlike most Anderson Shelters this one had not been covered with earth, thereby leaving the corrugated iron exposed, and it was getting warm. Very warm...

"What's that crackling noise?" someone asked, voicing the question in everyone's mind. The crackling noise wasn't loud. But, like, *sinister*. "This wall feels hot..." said someone, trying to be calm. 'The other side is stone cold...' Bewildered people, trapped in little more than a hole in the ground, covered by a corrugated iron roof and walls, trying to be brave in the face of adversity while some were feeling sick with worry inside.

One of the adults slipped out of the door and the crackling sound was louder. Quickly he returned and there was a voice shouting from the road end of the garden. "Come out quickly... run to me..." he shouted. "One by one, kids first, ladies next, .." It was an air raid warden. We obviously had to get out. Fast..

Out shot Tony, followed by me, followed by the grown ups. The hedge and the fence were on fire on our right as we ran up the garden path, illuminated by fire. The crackling sound was the branches of the hedge burning and the wind came from the other side, blowing the flames towards us and heating that side of the shelter that we were vacating at the double.

Single file, we were then led up the road and in that short journey we marveled at the night sky, lit up with the glow of a building burning profusely somewhere not too far away. In the background there were louder explosions as larger bombs found targets in this industrial inner ring of the old Birmingham. It's part of Birmingham's Balti Belt now, peopled mostly by Asian ethnic groups. Back then, though, most of us wouldn't have known what 'curry' was. And the only Indians, Pakistanis, Bangladeshis we'd ever seen were on black and white film.

The cause of our rapid retreat quickly became clear. The family who had vacated the house next door were motor cycle enthusiasts. Quantities of rubber tyres, half-full petrol tins and the like had been left in their outhouses which had received a direct hit from an incendiary bomb.

The wind blowing from that garden to the one next door, completed the picture. We'll never know whether we might have been incinerated, probably not, but this was war being fought on the streets of Birmingham, with the ordinary population on the front line. We had been dragged into world events and most people didn't really understand why.

My personal memories of the Birmingham Blitz are jumbled and fragmented. One dreadful night has blended into another to complete a mental montage of bombs, fires, searchlights, barrage balloons and wrecked buildings so that exact raids and precise dates are impossible to research.

Tony better recalls the unspeakable horror of it all, the fear that pervaded our sanctuaries whenever the bombs were close and getting closer. He remembers how it became so intense and persistent for a while that, rather than be plucked from our beds when the air raid siren woke us and chilled everyone to the marrow, we were simply bedded down every night in the Anderson shelter.

On another terrible night we 'all thought we were goners', Tony recalls. And when it was all over we were sure that, from the explosions we had experienced, buildings all around us must have been flattened. As the all-clear sounded we rushed out of the shelter and shouted back to the others that our house and the others nearby were still standing. Though only just it seemed...

The gate and gatepost were hanging loose, Tony recalls. Every window in every house around us was smashed and glass lay around everywhere yet, to our surprise, none of the houses around us were demolished. Only on closer inspection was it revealed that there was a crack in mom & dad's bedroom wall from ceiling to floor wide enough to push a finger into.

The crack was never mended in my personal memory but doors were put back on hinges by anyone who could help and, with national glass supplies exhausted, the shattered windows could only be replaced by strips of fabric. For a long time there was hardly a window to be seen anywhere near where we lived. Yet we seemed to cope, and in between the air raids, despite the loss of sleep, the ever present possibility of death and destruction, the shortage of pretty much everything you need, we still behaved like kids, and got ourselves, educated, too.

Strange to recall all these years on, when children are mostly reared in surroundings of some affluence or, at the very least, reasonable comfort, while deluged with a regular supply of toys at Christmas plus sweeties and other goodies all year round, Tony and I enjoyed few such luxuries in our upbringing.

With merchant ships the prime target of enemy submarines and other vessels the imports from abroad were virtually non-existent. This meant that we never saw, let alone actually devoured, such fruits as oranges, bananas, lemons and so on. One child brought a banana to school once, supplied by a relative who had been in the forces in warmer climes, and we all gazed at it in astonishment.

Sweets and chocolate were available sometimes, but very rarely and when one of our local shops, Mrs Cox's on the corner of Ansell Road and Golden Hillock Road and Mr Elton's in nearby Benton Road received a supply the word went round like wildfire and we all queued, ration coupons permitting, for a small quantity of whatever was available.

We only received the most basic and simple toys which meant that we made our own. A shoe box, with the open end on the floor and little 'doorways' cut along the edge and a number of points pencilled on top of each, produced a splendid target for a marble-rolling match.

Often we played marbles along the gutters on the way home

from school. Player 'A' rolled his as far as he could and then Player B rolled his to try and hit it. When successful you took your opponents marble and carried on like that, sometimes until one of you 'lost your marbles' and a catchphrase that caught on for generations meaning someone that wasn't quite all there.

We could make a toy 'tank', to go with our little tin soldiers, out of a used cotton reel, an elastic band, a small slice of candle fat, half a matchstick and a pencil. Thread the elastic band through the cotton reel and secure it at one end by threading the matchstick crossways through it. Pierce a hole through the candle fat and thread the elastic band through it at the other end,securing it with the small pencil fitted crossways like the half match stick.

Then wind up the pencil in a circular motion until the elastic band was stretched as much as it could be without breaking, place it on the floor and away it trundled just like a tank. Well, more or less. A great little toy. Cost? Nothing.

My personal favourite of all the makeshift toys was a pair of home-made stilts. Beg a line prop off your poor, old permanently harassed mother. Saw it in half. Then saw a small piece of the end of each half, screw them as footrests onto the longer piece of prop at the same distance on each....and hey, presto, a pair of stilts that you could walk around the road on, giving you the height to peer over hedges, fences and into windows that you otherwise couldn't. Magic.

Mostly, though, we played football or cricket in the street or across the nearby fields. We chalked a goalmouth on the wall of the house, split into two teams depending how many there were of us, and all tried to score into the same goal. Shots In we called it. Every few minutes we had to look each way to see if a copper was coming because they would clip your ear and stop you from playing if they caught you in the act..

Occasionally we had to clear a pile of recently-deposited horse manure from the road since most deliveries were by horse and cart...coal (when you could get it), bread and milk. The 'orse muck, as we called it, was popular with gardeners, though, so mostly it was collected, still steaming, as soon as a horse had unburdened itself. Dig for Victory was a famous wartime poster, and most of us did.

We got quite keen on growing Cos lettuces, radishes and other vegetables in the small areas of space not taken up by the air raid shelter. We also decided to keep hens, for egg production. Well, two to be precise. All we needed was a chicken coop, a chicken run, and some wire netting and this was where we could have been mistaken for staging an advance version of the famous post-war TV comedy, The Good Life.

The end brick-built outhouse, next to what we called the lavatory, or the lav, was emptied to accommodate the two birds, but it was pitch black inside and far too cramped. So we knocked a few bricks out on the garden side, opposite to the lav side, creating an opening wide enough for the hens to get in and out.

We then assembled every length of wire, every length of thin rope, every length of string, and even some lengths of strong wool, that we could muster and with the help of a corner upright hammered into the ground to form a fenced in corner area with the help of the outhouse wall and the garden fence, we had our chicken coop, and chicken run.

And WHAT an unbelievable hotch-potch it was! I can't even recall if we ever saw any eggs. Probably not. We ate the hens, more like, but I honestly can't recall exactly. If that episode has a strong humorous flavour to it, then it certainly was not funny when we were given a delightful little cocker spaniel puppy that instantly stole our young hearts.

Like for all kids, the thought of owning your own puppy

was just out of this world but - me being me, still as impatient now as I was then - I wanted it to grow up too fast. We took it to Sparkhill Park so that it could run about on the grass and then I had to see it swim. I put it into the boating lake in the park and though it clearly wanted to get out I left it in to doggy paddle at the side of the lake. That night it had a very dry nose and it had lost its spark. Soon after it was dead. I've always assumed that I got the little puppy too cold, too soon and for too long. I've never wanted a dog since.

Although generations of children had their lives fragmented by war in various ways described, the toys we received and the games that we played did not change too much during the six years of conflict. They were simple already before the war, and simple they remained.

There was hardly a street to be found in the inner ring of Birmingham or, probably, any other town or city where there wasn't at least one hopscotch grid to be found, marked out in chalk. There the girls gathered to play their hopping game. Standing nearby would be their baby dolls in the little prams and some would be alongside skipping away on the skipping rope that every girl owned.

In the roadway the lads were playing football or cricket, usually with a tennis ball, and breaking or just cracking a window now and again. Often the girls' skipping was a competitive game and sometimes there would be girl at each end of a lengthy rope twirling it around, and two or three would be skipping at the same time to see who could last longest.

Bicycles and scooters were regularly in use to keep girls active as were such old favourites as 'tag' and hide-and-seek. What they were NOT doing was sitting at home playing computer games, nor making up their faces and wearing fashion clothes like little adults, long before puberty, as some were to do later. A sight in pretty much every street back then, and for decades later, was that of full-sized prams outside front doors, in any weather, with baby well wrapped up and fast asleep in what passed for fresh air in the old industrial inner ring of Birmingham.

Babies didn't get snatched. Not a chance. Young children were perfectly safe and never threatened by adults in any way whatsoever. I was well into middle-aged, in the 1970s probably, before I so much as heard the word paedophile and even then I didn't know what it meant. Adults abusing children? Unthinkable.

In those far off days adults looked after children. They didn't abuse us. Well, yes, I know a few did but it was poor little kids at the hands of perverted relatives in their own home, not accosted by strangers in the street or groomed by monsters on the internet. And so the fact that we all had to walk to school, too, or travel by bike, no matter how long the journey, was never a problem, as long as we looked both ways before we crossed the road, and there was far less traffic to worry about.

If you travelled to school longer distances by bus, and there was a thick fogs, or an industrial 'smog' (a thick acrid mixture of smoke and fog), causing the buses to be taken off the road, you reverted to Shank's Pony as it was known. In other words you walked.

Schools never closed, whatever the weather, and there were some very harsh winters during the war. Being unable to get there because of bad weather was not even a consideration. We would have thought of ourselves as a nation of cissies to stay indoors just 'cos the weather was bad. And what one rarely saw were fat kids. Oddly enough the wartime diet and way of life had its compensations in more children than in later, more affluent and cosseted times, reaching their teenage years in quite good physical shape.

Sport played a big part in the lives of both Tony and me. The games in the road spread to cricket or football matches across the nearby fields bordered by Golden Hillock Road and half surrounded by factories on the far side towards Warwick Road.

Cricket was played with a discarded oil barrel for wickets, a bat heavily bound with adhesive tape to strengthen it and a hard ball. The rules were pretty basic. When the batsman heard a loud clang in knew it was out. If he knocked the ball as far as the ditch it was a four and if he cleared the ditch it was six. Otherwise runs were scored in the usual way, and there were some very strange bowling actions indeed.

As for football Tony became so keen that he actually formed a team of us kids and arranged a match for a group of us at King's Heath Park. I think at the time he had just started Grammar School, where rugby union was the sport, but 'footer' it was for us in our spare time, and Our Kid was always going to be the organiser.

Some of us had no proper gear, not even football boots. Mine were hand-me-downs, probably, and quite likely a size too big. I remember little about it except that as lads average age about 12 or something, playing on a full-size pitch, we had bitten off far more than we could chew. I do recall that, because no one wanted to play in goal, Tony persuaded me that I was just the boy for that job. It's easy Our Nipper, he assured me. No running around to be done like the rest of us. So in goal I went, aged about nine.

Standing at four-feet-something-or-other tall I stood under bar and looked up. I could hardly see it, let along jump up and touch it. And as for 'no running'...since there was no goal net I spent most of the time chasing after the ball each time it went past me.

No need to delve any more deeply into our schoolboy

sporting activities except to say that Tony went on to form a team which he called Sparkhill Corinthians, of which more later. One thing's for sure: we were taking on a love of sport with little help from anyone but ourselves and without expecting to be chauffeured around and spoon-fed, or to be provided with the best of equipment. We loved sport for the sport itself, and Tony was my mentor in that. It no doubt helped us both to progress to have career paths related to professional sport in a variety of ways... and, what's more, for our kid to become an international-class athlete.

For entertainment there were many picture houses (a bit posh to call them cinemas) within walking distance. Often they were 'A' pictures, for the over-16s only, unless you were with an adult...so you hung around asking strangers to buy your ticket for you. You promised to sit by them to watch the film, but obviously you never did. Quite often we would wait outside the exit doors until somebody came out and then, while the door was briefly ajar, nip in for nothing. The trick was to go straight into the toilet, which was near the door, so that the first the staff on duty saw of you was when you emerged from 'having a wee...!'

I remember when I got a little taller, but not much, I tried to get into an A picture on my own by wearing a trilby hat, a white silk scarf draped around my neck, and with a fag drooping out of my mouth. In my mind's eye I looked like Humphrey Bogart. As I was trying to say something like 'Ninepenny, please...' with the deepest voice I could muster, the cashier took one look at me, laughed, and sent me packing. Nobody laughed at Humphrey Bogart so I guess I must have got it wrong.

Funnily enough, though, for all its limitations, I don't remember it being a lousy childhood. What you've never had, you don't miss.

The Ansell Road street party to celebrate the end of WW2. Ma Shaw can be seen (front, seated left) with a plate of sandwiches.

A family wedding circa 1920. 'Dolly' Shaw is seated extreme left, front row. (the two ladies nearest to her on her left are thought to be her sister Annie and her mother. The next lady could be the third of the daughters, Ellen).

The author (right) with two RAF colleagues. 'We went into square-bashing as bewildered boys and emerged as fully-fledged airmen'.

Jim Norton at Norton Barracks, Worcester soon after his call up.

Frank Shaw (junior) in the Middle-East hell-hole of Aden in 1945.

Audrey (left) on the beach with friends, Eddy and Barbara Brown at the Scilly Isles in 1957. The previous year Eddy was Birmingham City's centre forward in the FA Cup Final against Manchester City at Wembley.

Frank Shaw's wedding to Winifred Woodcock. (l to r back row). Teddy's wife Lilian, Frank Shaw (senior) Teddy Norton, and Dunkirk survivor Norman Young. (Front row l to r) Ma Shaw and 'Big' Floss who died at 39 of breast cancer. (All those on the right of the picture are the bride's family and friends.)

Dennis (left), aged four, and Tony (6), celebrating the Coronation of King George V1, in 1937 outside the bay window of 21 Ansell Road.

Tony Shaw (2nd right, front row) in the Birchfield Harriers eight, pictured after winning both relays in the AAA Championships at White City. The front row comprises (l to r) Mike Rawson, a European 800 metres champion, Mike Farrell, and Olympic 400 metres athlete Johnny Salisbury. Second right (back row) is Peter Radford who set a 220 yards world record of 20.5 seconds.

Tony, second right front row, on parade in the RAF.

Jim Norton ready to carry out his signals duties in occupied France as part of the Normandy landings.

Ma Shaw with her second husband, Frank Shaw, 'maybe the best thing that ever happened to her'.

The Taylor family - George, Stan, Floss and Eileen, with toddler Audrey at the front.... while the Shaws were being bombed near the BSA, the Taylors were under threat as the Germans tried to hit the Dunlop and the Spitfire factory.

A 'sprog' at
the start of
square-bashing.
2526764 AC.2
Shaw.D is
extreme right,
front row,
kneeling.

Chapter 8
'...had I panicked I would have drowned'

We didn't get off to the best of starts after we had been deposited at our second evacuation 'home' in the village of Hartpury, Gloucestershire.

Finding ourselves back on the end of a crocodile of displaced kids once again we were the last to be accommodated at the very extremity of the village. It was the winter of 1940/41 and we evacuees were possibly the first factual illustration that the country folk had experienced that a war going on out there.

Perhaps some persuasive talk was necessary to convince our latest guardians to take us in but where else could we have gone? The teachers who had led us there couldn't very well return us back to our parents and say 'sorry, nobody wanted them' and the couple who took us in couldn't very well turn us away.

Two semi-detached cottages were set well back and we had lots of space at the side of the house.

Two of our teachers from Golden Hillock Road, Miss Haines and Miss Clews, were billeted next door but we rarely saw them . Our new temporary home was some sort of smallholding along the lane, some considerable distance from the village school though we arrived as darkness fell with no chance to look around and no idea what sort of people our surrogate mum and dad were to be.

She was very slim and dark with a busy, busy manner. He was typical of a particular kind of countryman, large, bulky and a man of few words, but not unkind. I can only picture him with a cloth cap on, indoors and out. His trousers were kept up both by braces and a wide leather belt.

We were sitting down at the table for our first meal, probably expecting meat, cheese, jam, or something like the food we would have had in limited quantities at home...but, to our horror, it proved to be just thick slices of bread, well covered in... lard.

I looked at Tony in sheer panic. There was no way, absolutely no way, that I could have eaten it. Tony neither. We must have sat there in total misery. Then Tony nudged my arm and I watched him break off a piece of bread and lard, as though he was going to eat it, but he actually dropped it under the table. Quick to catch on although only seven years old, I nibbled a little of the crust, broke off a bigger chunk, and dropped it under the table. Little by little we got through some of that opening 'meal', by nibbling half a mouthful, then dropping some more under the table.

Nearly seventy years on I can only imagine what it must have been like for that well-meaning, rustic couple when they realised what had happened. Slightly reluctantly I suspect, they had welcomed a couple of young endangered townies into their home, to share their meagre wartime rations, only to find their food and their good intentions scattered on the floor under the table.

After that is was never going to be a comfortable ride for either side. They didn't know quite how to deal with us and we were never quite at home being there but, at least, we'd been brought up from our earliest days to behave ourselves so we were never rude nor disobedient.

Unlike when we were at Worcester, going to school entailed what seemed to us a marathon trudge up a never-ending lane with the return trip to be undertaken a few hours later. Most of the other evacuees were billeted in cottages near the school and we never seemed to be part of their community any longer. We spent a lot of the time feeling hungry, too. On the first day were given bread and lemon curd sandwiches to take for lunch and when these met with our approval - unlike the bread and lard! - we were given them every day until we couldn't stand it any more.

After a while we just took to throwing them into the hedge once we were out of sight of our temporary home, leaving ourselves with hours and hours of rumbling stomachs until something else was put before us for our approval or otherwise.

Despite this unreasonable and ungrateful behaviour I've no recollection of being punished or deliberately treated badly by this couple that were probably as bemused by the unreality of it all as we were. It was simply that we'd been deposited there and we were more or less left to our own devices to look after ourselves. By normal standards I guess we were unintentionally slightly 'neglected" rather than ill-treated.

That was OK in normal circumstances, but rather tough on two young lads when the snow and freezing temperatures arrived. I can recall plodding through the snow to school in the morning, inadequately dressed, and heading shivering and blue with cold, for the nearest radiator when we got there to thaw out.

Soon I had chilblains on my toes caused by cold and damp and one of them swelled up and burst. . Not wishing to be a nuisance to our hosts I got myself a length of bandage from somewhere, bound it up, left it, and told no one. I've a vague recollection of the bandage getting increasingly grubby and the sore toe refusing to heal. I've still got the scar but I've also still got the toe so it clearly didn't rot and drop off...

I suppose we must have had baths and been kept reasonably clean though I can't remember there being a bathroom. There was a smelly outside loo, not far from an even smellier pigsty, I do remember that. Nowadays I see film of pigs being kept in clean sties with a concrete floor. These Gloucestershire pigs wallowed in deep mud and their own waste and you could smell them from yards away.

One of the bonuses was that we were at least out in the country, with ample space to run around and play, animals to be observed. I remember a beautiful chestnut horse with shaggy main in one of the fields and yearning to be taught to ride it. Roy Rogers, the singing cowboy of movie fame, and his lovely golden Palomino, Trigger, would have been nothing on us. Except that I had a voice like a young bullfrog with bronchitis.

That was official, by the way. On one of my earliest days at school just before the outbreak of war, the teacher set us all singing some simple song and went round the class, one by one, listening to us individually, brutally sending the five year old growlers to the front of the class to be exempted from future singing lessons. I was designated as 'a growler', so no career in singing for me then.

However, I digress. In a large barn where straw, seed and stuff was kept, a huge barrel of home-brewed, rough cider, or *Scrumpy*, with an enamel mug hanging from the spout, literally inviting visitors to try a mouthful or three. Tony and I could never quite decide whether we liked it or not but it didn't prevent us sampling it from time to time just to attempt to acquire the taste. Which, I suspect, though memory is rather blurred, that we did....transferring that affection later to good English ale, prepared in much the same way.

Tony recalls that we remained in Hartpury for only about five months, from October/November 1940 to around February 1941, so one Christmas was spent there, away from home. Mom and Dad visited us on Christmas Eve and brought our presents, Tony recalls, and ' it was the day that he realised that 'Father Xmas was a myth...!'

On the first week-end after the freeze arrived we ventured

into the nearby orchard which featured a small pond that was now frozen over into our very own skating rink, something I'd only seen in picture books with pretty girls wearing scarlet bobble hats and woollen scarves floating gracefully over the surface.

It was my turn now, and I stepped onto the ice. Or that was the intention. What I actually did was to step straight through it and into the cold water beneath, the surface of which briefly covered my head.

The duckpond wasn't particularly deep, but neither was I particularly tall. The impetus of stepping off the bank carried me just out of Tony's reach. When my feet touched the bottom, the surface of the water, now with segments of ice floating on it, was just above my head. Had I panicked I would have drowned but the instinct for survival must be embedded in the human psyche from the very earliest years.

From bent knees I sprang up like a jack-in-the box to get my eyes and, fortunately my nose, back into the freezing winter air. That was enough time for me to take a breath, see Tony running away from the poolside and to hear him shouting 'hold on...I'm getting a stick...' The next upward bounce enabled me to see him running back with a long branch is his hand, and by the third bounce, the end of that precious branch had reached me and I was pulled back the bank and hauled out.

Due to incredible presence of mind, for one so young, and instant action, Tony had saved my life.

Time now to pause and ponder what it must have been like for that country couple who had been kind enough, and sufficiently community-minded, to take in two unknown lads to save them from the bombs and here was one of them soaked to the skin, shivering from cold and a near-death experience and probably short of spare clothes to change into. In the absence of our parents, they were our official guardians, and therefore responsible for our well-being.

It must have been simply horrendous for them. Although my memory is not clear enough to be sure, it's a fairly safe bet that, with very few households having telephones in those days, we were expected to write home once a week to keep our parents assured of our good health and safety. If so, imagine what my letters must have been like in seven-year old handwriting, spelling and grammar.

'Got chill blane...ever so cold...I fell in the pond and nearly drowned...don't like the food...', or words to that effect. That, I confess, is pure invention but it might well have been the case and, in any event, it was not long after the pond affair before mom arrived at the door, with another member of the family, to take us home from evacuation for the second time.

There had been severe flooding on the journey, with the River Severn overflowing in Worcester and the Midland Red bus on which Mom was travelling having to drive through it with water up to its mudguards, frightening the life out of her. Seeing my toe bound up with a grubby bandage was the last straw for her. She turned to our lady guardian, whose name I can't recall, and said: "I'm taking them home." For poor old mom and dad it must have been the most agonising example of Hobson's Choice. 'Do we want to risk losing our two youngest by picking up live incendiary bombs ? Or by falling onto a duck pond?'

The danger of my drowning, experienced during evacuation – and of my parents losing their youngest child, just when they were taking significant steps to save him, and his brother – was repeated in even worse fashion on a wartime day out.

Again I'm unable to recollect full details other than what happened and where. Tony and I were with Mabel and her twin sons, David and John, and Beattie with her daughter little Margaret. They had taken us to a riverbank place on the Severn, near Bewdley, for some brief respite from the grimness of wartime life at home. The location will still be there, opposite a large outcrop known as Black Rock. There was a small area like a sandbank, ideal for a picnic.

It was popular with families with small children because they could make sand castles, of sorts, on the sloping riverbank and splash about on the edge of the water, where it was shallow. Margaret and the twins, were little more than babies, not even at the toddler stage, but I learned that if you pulled funny faces, did silly things or made daft noises you could make them chuckle. I liked that.

One such 'party trick', I discovered, was to attract their attention, pull a silly face, then roll down into the water, make a splash and wave to them. This was rewarded by chuckles from an appreciative audience. And the more it worked the more enthusiastic I became. So enthusiastic, in fact, that I rolled down the bank with such gusto that my momentum took me past the short safe area, and way out of my depth. Not good when you can't swim.

Logically, I guess, I should have drowned, sinking instantly into about twelve feet of water, going down slowly and being surrounded by air bubbles. Having gone down so far, (nowhere near the bottom, so I couldn't help myself like last time, by kicking up towards the surface) I started to rise again. Looking up, there was the outline of a bigger boy than myself, horizontal more or less, swimming on the surface right above me.

He'd been swimming in the water before I had decided to become a babies' entertainer, and though he wasn't in the water when I went in, he was now, and just as well for me, too. There was only that small boy between myself and drowning. Unfortunately, though, I was going down again. For some reason, either because I had been told as much, or had read it, I understood that if you fell in the water and couldn't swim, but held your breath, you went down and up three times before you drowned.

What I'm writing down here must have taken less than a minute, as long as the average child can hold his breath. To me, though, it was one of those 'time stood still' experiences. I don't think that my 'entire' life flashed before my but it was a close call, believe me. The second time I rose towards the surface my only hope was right above me on the surface. My sisters told me afterwards that when I disappeared from sight, they begged the lad to go back in and to look for me.

What a brave young man he must have been. How I wished I could have met up with him later in life to personally thank him for saving my life and risking his own. I wouldn't have survived without him, that's for sure. As I got towards the surface, and now presumably in the blind panic of desperation, I literally clawed my way towards him and grasped him around the neck. We could only have been a yard or two from the shallower bit so we were hauled by the adults to safety where I could gasp and splutter for breath. Fortunately I had not been in long enough to swallow much water and I must have recovered fairly quickly for the quite lengthy drive on the Midland Red bus back home.

During that dark period of world history our welfare was just a drop in an ocean of worry and anguish for those adults left behind on what was know as the Home Front while men of call-up age and women volunteers fought, got maimed or killed in various theatres of war. The blitz was still on when we returned from our second spell of evacuation but by then the Hun's own resources were stretched to breaking point by their battles on various fronts and we had them on the run and the bombing was coming to an end.

In desperation Germany's tactics were switched to the infamous doodle bugs that they rained on London and its surrounds. These were V1 and V2 unmanned flying bombs that were fired indiscriminately on the UK but could not reach further north then the South of England.

Some time after that Jim was in France having landed at Normandy as part of the follow-up battalions that flowed in after the D-Day landings, while Frank, who had been an ailing youngster I gather, was in the Royal Air Force, originally stationed at Wellesbourne, near Stratford-Upon-Avon.

Before his call up, and during the blitz, Frank would join the other able fellows who roamed the streets during the night, motivated by a mixture community spirit and a sense of adventure. He could help put out fires, rescue trapped casualties from bomb-blasted buildings, make himself useful as yet another blitz wreaked its havoc.

Prowling along Golden Hillock Road one night as the Nazi explosives rained down, he spotted an object dropping onto the roof of the school, the one he had himself attended ahead of us. Scaling onto the roof, with whatever implement he could lay his hands on, he contrived to scoop what proved to be an incendiary bomb off the roof above the classrooms and down onto the concrete pathway below.

Had he not been out there the school could have burned down. At assembly next day a delighted Miss Bearwood told the gathered children of the overnight report that she had received...Tony and Dennis Shaw's older brother, former pupil Frank, had saved their school so that they could continue their lessons. Good news, indeed...though not all of the kids were as gushing in their praise as the admiring Head Mistress.

Soon Frank was drafted into the RAF but I can't recall what his trade was, nor his duties at Wellesbourne. It's safe to say it that it was based on keeping our sorely-pressed aircraft in the skies whenever required. Later he was sent out to Aden, at that time a British Colony in the Yemen.

It was a posting at what was regarded as the worst possible hell-hole of deprivation for anyone not used to such unremitting heat. There had been a British presence in Aden for many years. The Gulf of Aden was a busy shipping line and strategically important to us. All I can recall is that when he was eventually sent home, invalided out of the RAF after a bout of rheumatic fever, he was a parody of what he'd been when he left home. I remember seeing him crossing the road towards our house after he had been invalided out.

His grey demob suit hung from his under-nourished frame, looking a size or so too big. Thin, pale, dark rings under his eyes, Frank never really recovered from his ghastly experience. No unprepared resident of Sparkhill, Birmingham, whose furthest journey until then was probably Blackpool, should have been unceremoniously dumped to live under canvas in a climate that wasn't fashioned by nature for white men. I'll always believe that his stay in Aden triggered of the dreadful events that were to overtake him later.

Chapter 9
'...Some of the bloodiest battles of the war took place there'

A flotilla of invasion boats left Newhaven Harbour to assemble in the Solent via Portsmouth for a channel crossing in the opposite direction to the one that had taken place in similar waters just after the start of the war four years earlier.

THEN the remains of a defeated army was being brought back from France to England from Dunkirk to lick its wounds, both physical and mental, to re-assemble and to grow once more into a fighting force.

NOW it was revenge time. On this return journey, however, the odds had shifted with the Allied forces aided and abetted by the USA, a different kettle of fish entirely. The Americans were heading for Paris and then Berlin and the Hun was not going to stop them. The Brits and our Allies were heading off to first liberate Belgium and Holland and then to aim to join up with the Americans in Berlin.

The boats were jam-packed with armed soldiers ready to reinforce the bridgehead established in Normandy by the D-Day landings and the occupants, deep in tense concentration already, were surprised and slightly alarmed to find that the rough, foam-flecked sea around the Isle of Wight was populated by what seemed to be hundreds of similar vessels.

"It's as crowded as Piccadilly Circus," said one of them as he studied a log-jam of vessels that gave the impression that it would be possible to walk from the coast of Hampshire to the Isle of Wight from one to the next without needing to swim. "We're sitting bloody targets for Jerry if he comes in by air." But Jerry didn't. Indeed, Jerry **couldn't**, with land and air resources reduced by the wastage of men and machines in the four years of fighting that had gone before, and at full stretch on various fronts.

Among those in the leading boat, the SS Canterbury, was 5254043 Sergeant James Norton a signaller of the 1st Battalion of The Worcestershire Regiment- our Jim - on his way to his contribution to a war that had swung heavily in the Allied favour ever since the Japanese had bombed Pearl Harbour resulting in all the might of America now being behind the all-out campaign to defeat the Nazi aggressors.

Japan would cop it eventually...but only after America had helped the rest of the Allied forces to put the Jerries in their place....

When the boats arrived in the waters off the French coast, after crossing in rolling seas that left every man suffering from sea sickness, Jim climbed over the side of the Canterbury as it approached the Normandy 'Gold' Beach, and shinned down a rope onto the deck of a landing craft to be taken to the shore to join the assault to push the Germans back, yard by yard, until they surrendered.

This should have been D-Day (June 6) +10 but embarkation had been delayed for several days by high winds and storm-tossed seas that made it far too dangerous to risk the crossing and it was June 22nd when the 26-mile voyage finally was completed. Waiting on the French coast for the landing crafts was an ingenious piece of equipment known as a Mulberry Harbour, positioned there by the advance party on the strength of a lesson well learned.

After a costly Allied raid on Dieppe in 1942, in which over three thousand Canadians were killed, injured or taken prisoner, it was realised by the chiefs of staff that no port on the coast of France would be taken by a frontal attack. The new plan was to land at a totally unexpected and remote location in rural Normandy, but to be sure that men and machines would not sink into soft sand.

That additional potential problem had been part of the

disastrous Gallipoli landing on the Turkish coast near the end of World War 1 when hundreds of Allied troops, Australians and New Zealanders mostly, had been bogged down and mown down by the strategically placed Turkish army lying in wait. One absolute imperative this time was to get off the landing crafts and off the beach as quickly as possible.

The portable harbours, which were towed across the Channel, were designed to have a life span of ninety days and to be capable of unloading 11,000 tons of supplies each day, while they worked to perfection for the main landings earlier, this one had been smashed almost to smithereens, the gales of the previous few days. While most of the men had to wade ashore waist deep, and begin their invasion soaked to the skin Jim, recalls. "I was dead lucky. There was a small part of the Mulberry Harbour still intact and I was able to step off the landing craft without even getting my feet wet..."

In their training, the signallers had been taught how to lay field telephone cables, how to relay messages by morse code or semaphore flags, the fundamentals of wireless messaging and carrying and using mobile radios, though they turned out to be worryingly unreliable. Now on French soil his job in his role as Platoon Sergeant, under the command of a Platoon Officer, Jim would supervise his fellows into laying cables ahead of the infantry to ensure communication between advancing units.

In a strange sort of way he regarded himself as 'lucky' to be there at all. Originally, a he had been among the vast number of young men being trained to join the British Expeditionary force that earlier had been sent to France to help keep the Germans at bay at the start of the war but which was left stranded and in retreat when the French quickly caved in and surrendered.

The BEF was driven back to the miraculous Dunkirk drama when thousands of them were at Hitler's mercy on the beach before being lifted by the streams of small boats that went across the channel from the south coast and the Channel Islands to pluck them from enemy territory. But for that heroic, Winston Churchill-inspired operation, there would have been no British Army and no defence of the realm. But thousands of young mean died in that debacle and Jim realised that he could have been one of them. His big mate, Norman Young, had been rescued off the Dunkirk beach by a small boat and returned home looking like a Zombie until he settled back into civilian life and became a school caretaker.

Jim's fortunate absence from Dunkirk derived from what proved to be a 'lucky' football accident. As Norton Barracks' goalkeeper in a football match during the build up to being sent to France, he went for a high ball collided with the opposition centre forward, who just happened to be Dennis Westcott, the Wolverhampton Wanderer's 1939 FA Cup Final centre forward. In the fall Jim twisted his knee badly, needed a cartilage operation, and by the time he was fit again the Dunkirk rescue mission had been completed thereby ensuring that his time was spent in training for the part he was to play as a signaller, including promotion to the rank of sergeant.

All that was history, however. Now he was on Nazi-occupied soil near the village of Mont Fleury and two days after landing they were charged with the duty of relieving the 15th Scottish Division who had landed with the early wave of men and weapons. The indomitable Scots had fought hard at the sharp end of the battle suffering heavy casualties near the little town of Cheux-Saint-Manvieux, approximately 10 kilometres West of Caen.

Some of the bloodiest battles of the war took place there. The Scots had taken some terrible punishment as the dead bodies, the burned out vehicles, the shell and mortar craters starkly illustrated to these frightened but courageous young soldiers as they mentally had to deal with the unimaginable terror of the eve of their first battle. Later, when hostilities were over, the Commonwealth War Graves cemetery located nearby became a lasting symbol of all those unfortunate souls who had paid the ultimate price.

In those opening days, Jim was kept back among a group of key personnel known as Left Out of Battle because casualties were always heavy among newcomers to the fray and the LOBS were not regarded as 'expendable' so early on in the campaign so his role was in a hastily set-up temporary Battalion HQ. First task was to dig themselves into slit trenches to prepare for a similar kind of horrifying warfare that had seen hundreds of thousands of soldiers from previous generations massacred in infamous WW1 battlefields like *Passchendaele*, the Somme and Ypres.

Now in 1944, a mere 30 years on, the lunacy was being repeated. One of the trenches, excavated to house a group of officers, received a direct hit by one of the shells and mortar bombs that rained over unremittingly, killing them all. The officer, in charge of Jim's platoon lasted only two days before he was withdrawn from the action, reduced to a trembling wreck, suffering from acute shell shock, thereby requiring Sergeant Norton to take his place as Acting Platoon Officer until a replacement arrived.

A trusty member of Jim's platoon, he recalled, was a black-haired young man when he arrived in France. When he entered the heat of the terrifying battle soon afterwards, his hair was said to have 'turned white overnight,' such was the mental stress they were under...yet he carried on with ultimate courage at the sharp end of the fighting right through to the end of the war.

Hill 112 wasn't really a steep hill at all, just a gentle

upward slope to an area of ground that was higher than its surroundings. From its elevated position, virtually all of the Normandy battlefields could be observed. For that reason it was strategically essential for the Allied forces to control it rather than allow the Germans to keep it as a means of delaying their retreat.

Two unsuccessful attempts had been made, by attacking via the flanks, to take out the nest of machine guns and other weaponry, backed up by tanks, that was taking savage toll of the invading army. Third time had to be 'lucky'....whatever the cost in men and munitions.

This almost suicidal, but crucial task was assigned to the 1st Battalion of The Worcesters whose platoon of signallers would have to go forward as inconspicuously as possible to lay lines of communications so that when the assault came each unit could tell battalion headquarters, and each other, the state of the battle from where they happened to be.

From these killing fields, The Worcesters, emerged triumphant and played a decisive part in many of the key battles en route through France, Holland and Belgium until the victory that defended the world against Nazi tyranny was completed. They were the first battalion to cross the Seine, at Vernon, in the face of very heavy resistance then pressed on to cross the road bridge at Nijmegan heading for Arnhem Bridge , but there they were sadly too late to save the remnants of the paratroopers whose audacious attempt to capture it had proved to be 'A Bridge Too Far....'.

Throughout that part of the campaign Jim was acting Signals Officer and only after the Seine crossing was he replaced. The morning of 18th November 1944 saw the 1st Battalion Worcestershire Regiment move across the Dutch/ German border to commence their attack on German soil in order to take the village of Tripsrath. As part of 214 Brigade they were the first British troops to fight on German soil. Their job was to take the north-west side of Geilenkirchen to cover the left flank and support the Americans.

The Regimental website describes how, when they set off on their latest mission, 'dawn broke with grey skies and heavy rain', fearful conditions in which to fight and press forward. As they approached the battlefield from which the defending Germans had been pushed back, the area was littered with corpses and the mangled remains of vehicles in a sea of squelchy, ankle deep mud.'

One officer reported later how he had been returning on foot to HQ alongside a six-foot high wall when he heard German voices on the other side. They were just a few feet from him but they didn't know he was there. Two enemy soldiers appeared to be arguing in loud voices, possibly through fear of the Allied advance.

The Worcesters officer unclipped a hand grenade from his belt, took the pin out with his teeth, mentally counted 'one-two' then tossed the grenade over the wall. "There was a loud bang, some screaming and then silence," he wrote. 'I carried on walking to HQ.." That, in a few seconds, summed up what the war was doing to the unfortunates whose unwanted destiny was to fight in it.

As the hours rolled by and the battle raged both sides suffered excruciating casualties as death and destruction took its inevitable toll. If the fiercely defending Nazi forces were to be pushed back, as pushed back they were, that's how it had to be as The Worcesters played their part in another victorious, if bloody and expensive, victory.

Thereafter, in what was devised by Field Marshall 'Monty of El Alamein' Montgomery and code-named Operation Veritable, the final stages of that particular part of the Allied offensive to free Europe was played out in a series of battles in which Sergeant Jim Norton, it appears, played a significant role.

On February 24th, 1945, he was successfully recommended for the Military Medal by Lieutenant-Colonel Hope-Thomson in a citation that read:

"Throughout Operation VERITABLE from 11th February 1945 onwards, Sergeant NORTON, the Signal Platoon Sergeant, set an example of devotion to duty and initiative that was quite outstanding.

On 16th February at BERKHOFEL after a successful attack by the Battalion, lines had to be laid to companies whose exact positions were still unknown. Under continuous and heavy shell and mortar fire of the whole area, this NCO led a line party, which worked all night and finally succeeded in establishing communications forward.

"By the time the battle reached IMIGSHOF on 18th February, the line section was becoming very tired, so he himself frequently went out, always under heavy fire, to re-establish contact with companies. This was done entirely on his own initiative, and reported to the Signals Officer only after the task was completed.

"The success of this series of operations was due in no small part to the maintenance of communications. Sergeant NORTON by his personal effort, initiative and courage during this very strenuous and trying period so helped to inspire his Platoon that operations never suffered for lack of communications."

Monty himself, no less, subsequently presented Jim with his gong, though he dismissed it as being an award for the brave signals platoon that he led as its Non-Commissioned Officer (NCO) rather than simply for himself. So many of his men, he insisted, had risked their lives again and again over a period of 12 months and more, without the recognition that they deserved.

He always regarded his Military Medal as a tribute to their collective courage in the face of shot and shell, hunger and hardship, sleepless nights and desperate days, more than a personal pat on the back, and he subsequently professed a profound impression that the system of the 'decorations', while a great honour to himself and others, was not fair to all of those deserving brave soldiers.

Some of his memories, from days long ago, when battles raged around them all, and human beings were forced to inter-act like aircraft on autopilot, are blurred and unclear. One mental image that never left him, though, was when this most compassionate of individuals was forced to shoot, in cold blood, a soldier from the other side.

Along with comrades he was defending a strategic position as enemy soldiers stealthily approached towards them, unaware that they were under such clinical surveillance. Jim had one of a group of four in his sights and could have pulled the trigger at any time. "Our instruction was always the same in this situation," he recalled. "Don't shoot until you can see the whites of their eyes..."

Jim's German attacker crept forward unwittingly until the silent death knell was sounded and the trigger was pulled. He had no doubt killed enemy soldiers before, but in the murderous maelstrom that slaughtered young men on both sides, with none quite sure whose bullets had been deadly, it just seemed part of the job. This one was different... "Uncomfortable thoughts crowd through your head," he declared sadly. "He was somebody's son. He could have been a husband like myself. He could have been a father..."

Even when hostilities were as good as won the misery dragged on for week after week. Mopping up operations had to be carried out. Comrades were killed right up to the moment that the once-mighty German war machine caved in and Hitler took his own infamous life skulking in his bunker well away from the murder and the mayhem that his madness had inflicted upon countless millions around the globe.

For much of the desperately cold winter of early 1945, when the ground temperature was officially recorded as at a record low, The Worcesters were camped out, living in slit trenches in the frozen ground and still exchanging fire with an enemy in its death throes. Near to their encampment were the parachutes that had been abandoned by allied paratroopers who had landed in support, and the silk proved to be useful lining for their slit trenches, those stone-cold holes in the ground that served as home sweet home for young men who had been fighting pretty much day and night for months on end.

For an added bit of warmth they would make impromptu oil lamps by pouring petrol into a tobacco tin, threading through some string to serve as a wick and thereby providing a rosy glow if no real comfort. At one stage they had captured Bremen, where they found the local population all too ready to give up the fight just as sections of their army had done. In his memoirs Jim recalls with a chuckle, an all-too-brief period when he was able, by kind permission of his signals officer, to enjoy very fleetingly, 'the spoils of war...'

"Sergeant Norton!" he was ordered. "Come with me."

He was led a few hundred yards down the road to a Mercedes-Benz car showroom that had been abandoned and was deserted. "Help yourself," he was told by his officer. And they both drove off with a stylish model of the iconic motorcar, a small reward, it must have seemed, for all that they had been put through. But the 'Merc Owner' status did not survive for long. The next time he wanted to go for a drive it had disappeared. Someone had nicked it...." All's fair, it seems, if not in love, then certainly in war.

Happily, soon afterwards, came the news that they had all been waiting for. At one of the great moments in world history, the officers were having a meal in a dining room they had established for themselves. A signals sergeant had received a message from Battle HQ. He knocked politely on the door of the Officers' Mess, coming smartly to attention as he was called in. And he then announced in the clearest of tones to the assembled, uniformed diners: ***"Gentleman. The war is over...."***

And so, apart from a bout of concussion caused by a flying brick as a makeshift battalion HQ, where he was working was shelled, Jim emerged from the battlefields of Europe virtually unscathed. Not only was he a brave and efficient soldier, he proved to be a lucky one, too.

Chapter 10

'...we would discuss what sins we had committed so that we had something to confess'.

The war in Europe officially ended on May 8, 1945, as Germany surrendered unconditionally soon after Adolf Hitler's partly burned-out body was found in his bunker. Roughly three months later, after atomic bombs had been dropped, first on Hiroshima and then on Nagasaki, the war in the Far East ended, too, as Japan also surrendered unconditionally on August 15th.

On each occasion, first VE Day and then VJ Day, the UK virtually became one big street party and I can well remember mother being part of the arrangements for ours in Ansell Road. A lengthy trestle table was erected, covered by table cloths borrowed from houses that could produce them, and the table was then laid with whatever celebratory food could be mustered collectively.

There's a black-and-white picture still in existence of mom, sitting on the kerbside by the table with a huge plate of sandwiches that she had cut, a symbolic image of Ma Shaw, who had no doubt also contributed the odd jelly or blancmange to make sure us kids had a dessert. By then, and some time during the war, though I can't remember when, she had started working at the BSA, operating a lathe that would have been a man's job in peacetime. She was prepared to work in a factory, presumably to help send Tony and I to Grammar School, but she maintained a sense of pride that some factory workers had either discarded or never possessed.

She always went to work wearing a smart coat, hat and shoes and she always hurried home at lunch time if Tony and I needed some 'dinner', as we would have called it. When she did she walked tall, with head up and shoulders back. There must have been a dreadful fear in her mind that she might be regarded as 'common' because she worked in a factory. Her unshakeable sense of what was right and what was wrong remained intact to survive those six years of mostly misery laced with occasional pleasure. Time now, she may have decided, for any guilt she felt at not exposing her two youngest to the Roman Catholic religion, on which she had been reared, to be removed.

Already she had stepped outside of the faith by marrying a non-catholic and so, presumably to balance the books, as it were, Tony and I, along with our two friends from nearby in Barrows Road, were eased into the opportunity of a Roman Catholic lifestyle. We had been christened as Catholics but by the time we were old enough to start going to church other influences were in place. Six years of World War for example.

Dad not being a catholic must have had something to do with this. In any event our local church, between Walford Road and Benton Road, was Church of England. We used to go there, to Wolf Cubs, with church services involved so we'd already set off on the 'wrong' religion. However, when the war was over, and Dad's health was starting to fail, we started to get visits from Father Bird, the parish priest from the English Martyrs catholic church near Sparkhill park, baths and library.

I remember him as a lovely, gentle gentleman who would give our protestant , unwell dad the price of a jug of beer to be fetched from the 'Blue Brick' a Mitchells & Butler off-licence, on Golden Hillock Road, opposite Walford Road, while presumably doing his duty as a catholic priest in advising Mom that she and her two lads should attend his church.

This led to Tony, myself, Garth and Rex from across the road becoming regular, week-end churchgoers. It was maybe a mile and a half each way and, since cars were then not an achievable tool of the common man, we walked it, quite early each Sunday morning. It wasn't only Sunday morning, though, as it turned out. Very quickly the routine became Confession every Saturday morning and Communion every Sunday morning. As every catholic knows (that's if it still applies and I'm not sure if it does) for a period of time between confessing your sins and then receiving redemption from them, God's child is not expected to eat.

I believe that communion was normally taken, say, once a month, or even once occasionally or even as an obligation at Easter time and otherwise only when it felt appropriate. That didn't apply to us four escapees from the blitz. Possibly because we had some catching up to do we went pretty much every week for a while. I honestly can't remember how long that period was except that Mom had said that we could make up our own mind on how, and how often, we would worship once we had started work. For now, like it or not, and I didn't, we were to be weekly regulars.

Just to give a flavour of what it was like, I can recall quite clearly one particular Saturday morning. On the way to church the four of us would discuss what sins we had committed so that we had something to confess. That process wasn't easy. We were well-behaved kids, for heaven's sake, in the 11 to 14 age groups with precious little opportunity to misbehave. Chance would have been a fine thing, as they say, and we couldn't very well say 'I haven't committed any sins, Father'. No point in going. In any case the religion seemed to be based on the surmise that we're ALL unworthy sinners.

There was a menu of sins to choose from some of them - such as not going to church at Easter - that were so terrible that unless you got yourself cleansed by prayer and ultimate forgiveness, that you would never have been admitted into the Kingdom of Heaven. I decided that among my pathetic little misdemeanours, I would say that I had been 'unclean in thought and word'. Not thought, word and **deed,** mark you. Just 'thought and word'. Possibly, as an 11/ 12-year-old whose only knowledge of the facts of life was what I'd picked up in the playground, and dismissed as far too rude to be real, I'd looked at some little girls knickers, wondered what was underneath, and talked about it to an equally perplexed pal i.e 'thought' and 'word'.

So when my time came to enter the confessional, I knelt on the cushion beneath the metal grill window that was covered by a black curtain, through which the silhouette of Father Bird could easily be recognised. And, of course, his voice. As a really nice man who'd bought beer for my ill dad when mother couldn't afford it, I wouldn't want to appear to him to to be a really bad boy.

'Bless me Father for I have sinned...' I began, in the manner we had been taught.

'Bless you my child...' he responded along with whatever came next in order to extract from me the depths of my depravity.

'I've been unclean in thought, word and deed...' I responded, no doubt committing another sin in mentally cursing my mistake. (Oh! no...not **deed** as well, you daft *******)

Normally, on getting our week's crime sheet off our chest we were given two or three prayers to kneel and say before running that mile and a half back home to get some food inside us at last... having been starved, remember, since some time the previous day. This time though Father Bird must have been shocked to hear that little Dennis had been 'unclean' not only in thought and word but in 'deed', too. In hushed tones I was instructed to go back into the body of the church and say something like 20 'Our Fathers' and '20 Hail Marys' and whatever else as instant penance, while contemplating and praying for forgiveness for whatever dastardly deed it was that, in error, I had unintentionally 'confessed' to having committed.

Give my brother and our two mates their due they dutifully waited outside with me, probably waiting with glee, and possibly envy, to discover what the heck I had been doing to deserve such heavy-handed punishment before, on the race home, contemplating our austerity breakfast dredged from the ration allowance. Fried spam and dried egg, probably.

Here it's maybe timely to report that I've been increasingly less religious ever since, and a non-practising Roman Catholic most of my adult life. All I will say is that if there truly IS a God, then he's been extremely unkind to lot of people I know who don't deserve it and far too kind to others, who equally don't deserve it. He didn't do much for our mom, that's for sure.

Now back to those early post-war days, it would be pleasant to recall that, having by now had ten years of her approximate 50 years, taken up by those two world wars, that peacetime would be kind enough to bring with it comfort and contentment. Sadly those early years after hostilities finished, produced, along with some joy...only yet more struggles.

Dad had been a smoker for much of his adult life, as had been a high percentage of men, and this presumably contributed to what proved to be terminal cancer. I know dad received about £350 pounds down-payment from a superannuation scheme when he had retired at 63 in 1946, two years early. It was a fortune to them at that time but it would soon run out and in 1948 Ma Shaw's second husband died leaving her with very little visible means of support. It was said at that time that she wasn't a very good 'money manager' but I don't think she'd ever had much to manage.

Through contact with a niece, (one of sister Annie's daughter's 'young Annie') who had a second-hand clothes shop in Ladywood Road, opposite the Birmingham Children's Hospital, she started a stall in the Birmingham Rag Market in Jamaica Row, off Bradford Street. World War 2 had ended, but the food and clothing shortages did not. Nor did life in Britain return to anything like normal, though it did improve gradually.

By this time Tony and I were benefiting from what to my dying breath I will regard as a double gesture of parental sacrifice unequalled in my personal experience. During that period of almost unbearable fear and uncertainty that prevailed for six long years, our mom and dad contrived to pave the way for us to go to a then fee-charging Grammar School. Very few families around where we lived even considered their children's education beyond the fact that they needed to be prepared to start work, most likely in a factory, by the time they reached fourteen or fifteen.

Yet there was Tony, in 1941, and myself in 1944, going off to school in the uniform of King Edward V1, Grammar School, Camp Hill, having somehow managed to pass the entrance examination despite our two evacuations to strange schools and all those nights in air raid shelters when we should have been asleep in our beds. Eight members of our family before us had settled for what was known as an 'elementary school' education. In contrast Tony and I were privileged to be afforded something a little better...and while it totally shaped our future for the better it took us into a world of contrasts.

With dad's health ailing, and severe bronchitis taking its toll, mom had to find a way of paying our annual fees until, mercifully, they became free schools not too long after the war. And find a way, she did. She discovered that discarded clothing, clean and in pretty good shape, could be obtained by knocking doors in the more affluent outskirts of Birmingham.

These could be sold by hiring a stall at the Birmingham

Rag Market in Jamaica Row, though therein lay a snag for Tony and I. The market operated on a Saturday. Mom needed helpers to carry her bundles of used clothes, travelling on foot and by 'bus, from Sparkhill to the edge of Birmingham to set up the stall and to help sell the goods. That meant us two, and how I absolutely hated it. One Saturday sticks in my mind and is maybe a reminder that being sent to mix at Grammar School with lads who hadn't been brought up in the industrial inner rung of Birmingham, had given me boyhood delusions of grandeur.

I'd been chosen to play for the school under-14 team at rugby. Our teacher who took us for rugger and cricket had told the school head of sport that I was a brave little tackler who 'could stop an elephant in full flight'. On that recommendation my name went on the notice board as being selected for the under-14s but, with a heavy heart that I thought might break, I had to ask to be excused for family reasons. (You can bet I didn't say I had to go to the Rag market to sell old clothes...). That wasn't all. Part of the route along which we had to walk with bags of second-hand clothing on our shoulder, and wait at the bus stop for the No.37 or some such, to Jamaica Row, was the very route along which buses travelling in the other direction headed for the school sports ground.

It was around the time when dad, aged 64, was dying that his daughter, Big Floss, a skilled seamstress and until then a lovely, cheerful, 39-year-old, who had physically deteriorated and shed weight alarmingly, tearfully let it be known to her sisters that she had a lump on one of her breasts.

Maddeningly, but for what she felt was the right reason, and with little knowledge of what it was all about, she had told no one, until then, because of the worry over her dad's declining health. She was whisked off to hospital by her two sisters Mabel, whom she lived with, and Beattie. But it was far too late. She died in October 1948, six weeks before our dad, both with cancer. Predictably our mother was tending them at their bedside when each of them took their last breath.

Yet, during those years of pre-war teenagers in the mixed family reaching adulthood and getting married (no such thing as 'living together unmarried then, by the way) our family grew and grew. A year before the outbreak of war, in 1938 on my fifth birthday, Ivy and Syd had a son, Roy. They lived in a terraced house in Anderton Park Road, not far from where I was born on Coventry Road. Mom, Tony and I were there with other members of the family, gathered downstairs awaiting the arrival of their first grandchild. I was to be a five-year-old uncle, as birthday present I was told.

The whole thing was a mystery to me. Adults talked in whispers on the subjects of babies and where they came from. I'd gleaned that there was one on the way but just how would it arrive? No idea....

Suddenly there were smiles all round as the faint sound of a baby crying drifted from the room above. It's a boy, someone came downstairs to tell us. I didn't know where it came from but it was a darned good trick....No one had come through the door from the street with it, I was sure of that, and there was no hole in the roof for it to have fallen through. Clever.

The next children to arrive, as I recall, were a nieces. Teddy and Lily had twin girls, but only Valerie survived. Margaret was born to Beattie and Tom and then Mabel and Harry had twin sons, David and John. Later Frank and Winnnie had young Frank while and Jim and Brenda had first Keith and then Carl. Florry, who was known as Little Floss because of a half-sister, the one who died of breast cancer, also being named Florence and known as Big Floss, married a much older man in Bill Brown, and they had no children.

So, suddenly there were babies and toddlers in every branch

of the family and it came as a big, big surprise to me to discover how much I loved seeing them, and playing with them, and watching them progress in what they could say and do as they got older. Little lads can start off thinking that babies and all that is cissie stuff, but I quickly learned differently.

However, I digress. For the two servicemen in our family at the end of the war, their future was very different. Jim returned home to start off a very successful career in what was then known as Personnel, and later Human Resources. For his half-brother, Frank, though it wasn't so rosy. Far from it...

The doctor advised him that because of the state of his health after his term in the punishing heat of Aden, he should not return to the factory job for which he'd served as an apprenticeship before the war. But with no other qualifications what should he do? He was a shadow of the young man who went away, as much a war victim as any of those injured in armed conflict.

Now the father of young Frank, he set off as a part-time barman near the centre of Birmingham and then accepted the opportunity to become a licensee of a very poor pub on the corner of Gooch Street and Longmore Road in Balsall Heath, basically a slum area that became renowned for prostitution and petty crime and later became the very heart of Birmingham's Balti Belt. Now there's a mosque near where it once stood.

There he mixed with the wrong people, got into money trouble, disappeared for a while, lost the pub and was pretty much a broken man when, around 1950-51, he was re-housed in a poor quality dwelling in Summer Road, not far from the centre of Birmingham and not the future he had envisaged for Winnie, himself and their son.

I had started my two-years National Service in the Royal

Air Force, on August 14, 1951, a period when the Cold War with Russia was still on but, for the Home Front, the after-effects of WW2 were starting to fade. On a week-end pass one Saturday evening I was returning to 21 Ansell Road with some bottled beers from the Ansells outdoor on the corner of Benton Road and Osborne Road when I saw a car outside our house with its headlights on full beam. Strange ....

I hurried towards it and quickly realised it was a police car. A policeman and policewoman were knocking on the front door. I arrived there at precisely the time that Mom opened it. "Mrs Shaw they asked? "Do you have a son named Frank Shaw ? Can we come in?" The four of us were then crammed into the tiny hallway. "I'm sorry to have to tell you this, Mrs Shaw." one of them said. " Your son has been found dead. He committed suicide..."

I gasped and looked at Mom. "Oh! No..." she said. And her legs crumpled into the start of a faint. Then, fortified no doubt by similar past experiences, she straightened up. "Put the kettle on, Dennis," she said. "We must give them a cup of tea." When the tea had been drunk and the police car had left, Our Mom became Ma Shaw: pick yourself up, dust yourself down and start all over again. "We must go and see Winnie." We walked to the bus stop in Walford Road, caught a No.8 bus to somewhere or other, changed to another and walked down Summer Road.

Winnie answered the door, red-eyed and shell-shocked. "We were going out tonight," she said. "I'd gone to have my hair done.," She pointed to the gas cooker in the corner, standing on a red, flagstone floor.

"When I came home I could smell the gas. He was lying there,"she added as tears returned. The cooker door was open. There was a cushion lying in it. The three of us stared at the cold, hard area of flagstone where Frank had voluntarily ended his life. Nobody said very much, though the same thought was no doubt going through our mind...

What mental anguish must he have been suffering to prefer an end like that to the prospect of living on...We had no answers...except, perhaps, that the after-effects of that lousy, rotten war had wrecked our Frank's life.

Chapter 11

'The news pouring in, the urgency of everyone involved, the vibrancy of being part of a team, the constant deadlines'

Our kid knew exactly what he wanted to do when he left school so when mom explained that, with dad's enforced early retirement, and declining health, he would have to start work rather than continue his education into a fifth and final year, it was to the bigger of the two local newspaper groups, The Birmingham Post & Mail to which he applied.

I hadn't a clue about what I wanted to do to earn a living when I left school but in those days it wasn't a problem finding something. The broadsheet evening newspaper had page after page of Situations Vacant. You could probably have changed jobs almost every month if you wanted to.

In contrast Tony had not a single doubt. He wanted to be a sports journalist, hence his application for an opening as a trainee in the sports department of the Birmingham Mail. As it turned out there wasn't a suitable vacancy at that time so, instead, he accepted the chance to work in the advertising department with the proviso that if an opening eventually cropped up on sport he could move over.

Unfortunately for him that chance never came. What did turn up was a lucky chance for me, before I had even left school. Tony had a Saturday afternoon job on the Mail's Saturday night's Sports Final, sitting in an office taking down reports and scores on the telephone in pencil, written in long hand. Copy takers they were called and they were situated in offices located in the maze of corridors in the old Birmingham Mail building that saddled the corner of New Street and Cannon Street at the end of Corporation Street.

The part-time job he set up for me when I was 13/14 – taking his big brother role as seriously as ever - was as a runner on Saturday afternoon, hurrying from office to office, up stairs and down stairs, picking up the sheets of copy, taking them to the sports sub-editor's department, and then doing the rounds again.

Anyone who has lived only in the age of the computer and the mobile telephone will find it difficult to comprehend on one hand how basic it all was and on the other hand how quick and efficient it proved to be. The presses were rolling out copies of the Mail Sports Final, and the Birmingham Gazette and Evening Despatches 'Sports Argus' every Saturday night in the football season less than half an hour after final whistles had sounded all around the region.

That remember was with pretty much clapped-out old pre-war machinery backed up by a distribution service comprising old vans making their way through crowded streets. Oddly, and I've never understood this, the more that the system was 'modernised' and computerised, and the more roadwork networks improved, the slower the system became. They call it progress....

However, the experience did two things for me. It gave me ten bob a week pocket money (not bad then, 50p in new money!) and it gave me the taste for newspaper work. The news pouring in, the urgency of everyone involved, the vibrancy of being part of a team, the constant deadlines, the realisation that empty pages had been filled with information and the chance to see things you'd been involved in, instantly in print. It's a feeling I've never lost. It gives me a buzz writing about it even now, some 65 years later.

So now I knew what I wanted to be. I wanted to be a journalist and here, through Tony's help , I had an advantage over him. On his advice, when mom inevitably told me that I had to leave Grammar School because dad's health wasn't getting any better, I applied to the Evening Despatch rather than the Mail, was instantly interviewed by the Chief Sub-Editor, Cyril Ticquet, and started as a messenger boy in the editorial department on April 5th, 1948, two days before my 15th birthday.

Our interest in sport had been fermented by dad and my three brothers from the time we were old enough to listen to their stories before we'd even started school. Aston Villa was their common footballing love and we were told of Pongo Waring's amazing goalscoring exploits, Eric Houghton's thunderous shooting and unstoppable penalties, the brilliant little Frankie Broome, my personal hero, the reports and pictures of it all every Saturday night.

We heard all about Wembley Stadium, the White Horse Cup Final when the fabulous new ground opened in 1923 and couldn't contain the crowds, all the football news every Saturday night in the Sports Argus, printed on pink paper. A *pink* newspaper? I couldn't wait to see that....

During the latter war years, when there was some organised football to fill in until the real stuff returned, Tony and I went to Villa Park on as many Saturdays as possible. The bonus there was that, because Birmingham City's ground at St Andrew's was unusable as the main stand had been burned down, the Blues played their home matches at Villa Park.

Sometimes we didn't have the admission price, even though it was only a few coppers for kids, but they opened the gates, free admission to all-comers at half time, and that's when we nipped in, our autograph books in our pockets.

Inevitably we became 'fans' of both clubs, but when they played each other Villa was our team. They say that true supporters are born to follow that particular club. It's true. We were born and brought up to be Villa fans but with a difference...if Blues weren't playing Villa we 'supported' them, too.! After six years of what we'd probably had enough of hatred. It never occurred to us to dislike anything in football.

When the opposition had a good move, or scored a goal against you, everyone clapped politely. The Villa park crowd prided itself on its reputation for sportsmanship.

Cricket came into our lives in a particularly privileged way. In order to get things going as quickly as possible when the conflict was over, Warwickshire County Cricket began running Festival Weeks at Edgbaston. Many of the players had lost six years of their careers due to the war and were simply glad to start playing again while many more were still in the forces but could get time off. The biggest bonus of all was that members of the Royal Australian Air Forces were still based in the UK, as were some of the West Indian players, so we saw some of the most exhilarating cricket imaginable during that period.

There was no easy way by bus so we walked there. I especially remember seeing legendary players such as Keith Miller, Denis Compton, Bill Edrich, Learie Constantine, Frank Woolley and heaven knows how many more. Tony and I had most of these and many other autographs of famous cricketers in a collection but at some stage threw them away ! We whittled out very wooden small bats and devised a cricket game to play on the floor of the house, using a marble as a ball. Tony was Bill Edrich. I was Dennis Compton. Boy, did it hurt when you missed the 'ball' with your bat and hit it with your knuckle.

Incredibly, Mom also allowed us to devise a boxing ring in the sitting room so that we could have boxing matches, our fists bound up with bandages and whatever to act as gloves. Can't remember Tony's name but I know I was Kid Kane. Mom had to stop it in the end. Can't think why...! Here again our dad and brothers had told us about Joe Louis, Jack Dempsey, Tommy Farr, 'Boy' Boon...the names of pre-war boxers who made us want to try it out for ourselves.

Athletics and cycling was also introduced into our lives in the early post-war years. In those days the large companies such as BSA, Lucas's and others, held annual sports days with a whole range of activities, some of them featuring high-class athletes from the likes Birchfield Harriers, and Small Heath Harriers and international-class cyclists. Tony and I couldn't get enough of it... and it didn't do us any harm.

The contrast between young people involving themselves in sport then, compared to later 'more sophisticated' years, could not be much wider. In those early post-war days of acute austerity there were few facilities, skeleton governing bodies, little money in people's pockets and hardly any sports shops selling equipment (even if we could have afforded to buy it, which we distinctly couldn't.)

Against that background , and with almost nothing going for him, Tony decided to start a football team. As you do! As a one-man organising committee he entered it into the Birmingham City Council JOC under18 League and took out a permit with the Parks Department to use a notorious 'black patch', grassless pitch at Calthorpe Park, in the heart of Balsall Heath near our brother Frank's pub.

It was the only pitch available, probably because no one else wanted to play on black gravel that scraped the skin off your knees if you fell on it, as we did. He registered our colours as 'Red' despite the fact that none of us had a red shirt. This small matter was overcome by everyone being required to secure a white shirt of any design, and take it to Tony who informed our mom, bless her, that she had to dye them all red, which she did with the use of a large iron pot. Had it been feasible he would have had them dyed claret and blue, to match Aston Villa, but even our mother couldn't achieve such a miracle.

The rag-tag collection of shirts came out looking a bit

streaky but they were red and, as I recall, we were quite proud to trot out all wearing the same colour shirt, even if our short and socks didn't match and many of us, including yours truly, have second-hand boots that didn't fit. To select a name, he had read the exploits of a well known great amateur team in the late 19th century known as the The Corinthians. Well, OK so we were distinctly 'amateur' and we were going to be 'great' weren't we, so Sparkhill Corinthians Football Club was born.

Tony recalls that we lost our first match 4-0, which wasn't bad. I can't remember anything about it apart from the awful pitch, often with large stones and even half house-bricks on it. I do vaguely remember a well-worn 'caseball', as they were called which we inflated and laced up at home. That was almost certainly the only ball we had. Nothing we had at that time was new.

We always had great difficulty in pushing the teat inside the aperture after inflating it with a bicycle pump. Often in trying to do so we punctured the inner tube ...so out came the puncture repair kit and we started again. The finished article, at the best we could get it, was more or less round but with a distinct bulge where the laces were located...not much fun to head when travelling at speed, I can tell you.

Away matches would have been on slightly better pitches and with a rounder ball but I'll bet the opposition didn't enjoy coming to our ground at Calthorpe Park. No place for nambie, pambies that's for sure.

We had to travel everywhere by bus, or tram, and on bad days, the return journey was undertaken with top clothes worn over the top of wet, muddy bodies. In many cases there were no dressing rooms at all and I don't recall any of them having showers. If you got badly injured it was, as we say in Brum 'tuff'.

One game I played in for the Evening Despatch after

leaving school, for instance, was at a park in Erdington. I was running along the left wing chasing a pass from defence and the full back was coming towards me to make a tackle. However the ball ran out of play before he needed to make a tackle but as I bent down, out of the playing area, to pick it up he came flying in with the tackle anyway and hit me on the left shoulder with full force.

Because my shoulder hurt, I tucked my left hand into the waistband of my shorts and played on. At half time there was nobody around who knew about injuries but at the end of the game the park keeper came up to me and said he had seen me running around the pitch with may hand tucked in my shorts and thought that, on the way home, I should pop into the General Hospital in Steelhouse Lane for an X-Ray.

This I did after a journey into town on a tram that was shaking all over the place to my increasing discomfort. After a lengthy wait in a long queue at the hospital I was X-rayed and then told that I had fractured my clavicle (collar bone). Makes you think, doesn't it, when you see, at the time of writing, how multi-millionaire, professionally trained, fit-as-a-flea footballers roll about 'in agony' now because they've fallen over, poor dears.

Sport wasn't the only activity that we went for at any opportunity once the shackles of war had been released. Music was another part of popular culture that beguiled us. Music and dancing,

There had been music during the war and not only Vera Lynn and her morale-boosting songs of 'meeting again' and not knowing 'where or when', and 'bluebirds' being 'over the White Cliffs of Dover'. Big band swing from the 1920s and thirties whetted our appetite as did traditional jazz. We wanted more of that....

We had heard big bands...Glen Miller, Duke Ellington,

Tommy and Jimmy Dorsey but how could we actually SEE them, or bands like them. One of Tony's favourites was Billy Ternent and his Orchestra. In fact the opportunity to experience it all at first hand came in a most unexpected way in the late 1940s, A cinema, the Odeon, Warley, at the start of the Wolverhampton New Road on the Birmingham outskirts, began a series of Sunday night concerts FREE of CHARGE.

We would catch a bus into Birmingham and then the Quinton 9 from Colmore Row and make our way there. I'll never lose the image in mind of the first time we clapped eyes on the band assembled on stage, but I can't remember which one it was. It could have been the *Squadronaires*, an orchestra made up of professional musicians who had been serving in the RAF. Vic Lewis, who played 'progressive jazz' like the American big band , Stan Kenton, was one of the regulars. (Not my cup of tea, really, though Peanut Vendor is one of my all-time favourites.)

The whole stage was filled with musicians, set out in orderly fashion in their sections with their instruments, the brass section's trombones and trumpets gleaming in the stage lights, silver saxophones similarly glowing, rhythm section crouched over drums and double base, huge grand piano, ebony black on one side of the stage.

They looked, and sounded, quite magnificent, all bedecked in matching tuxedos and bow tie, trombone section standing to play their part of the arrangement, all pointing in the same direction before sitting down to give way to the saxophones, then a piano solo, a drum solo, vocalists adding the words and emotions.

Tony and I, and our two mates Garth and Rex were well and truly hooked. Some time later we went to jazz concerts at Birmingham Town Hall and in a different kind of way the Humphrey Lyttletons, Freddie Randles , Kenny Balls and their generation of fine British jazz musicians were equally magnetic to us. Then there was the dancing. We were taught ballroom dancing when I was a mere fourteen at a youth club that we started at Conway Road School, Sparkbrook, as a means of providing an entertainment and activity base for us kids who had been deprived of so much for six years.

Getting to actually hold a girl with an emerging adult figure while we moved to music and learned slow-slow-quick-quick-slow....and one-two-side-together with all its variations for the waltz, the quickstep, the slow foxtrot and the South American dances that I loved...samba, cha-cha and even the tango, was heady stuff for kids like us. Better than being blitzed, that's for sure.

It led to us swapping the picture house for local dances of which there were many, several in schools halls, others in local barracks halls, occasionally an actual ballroom. This was all before rock-and-roll, the obsession with the guitar sound, the emergence of the small groups, the strange urge to dance without holding the girl. How boring and embarrassing is that? Dancing alone...In our younger days you spotted the girl you would like to dance with. When the band, or the record, started up you walked across to her, and politely asked: "May I have this dance, please?" Courtesy dictated that the girl agreed with a sweet little smile, whether she liked you or not.

Then, for some reason, the necessity to talk to the girl arose. It wasn't enough to just hold her as close as decency permitted. You had to attempt to portray a personality which, I for one didn't find came easily, at the age of fourteen or fifteen with an inborn shyness of girls. A shyness of everyone, probably.

Standing about five feet tall, not long out of short trousers, no sign of a whisker on a smooth chin, (designer stubble? I wish...bumfluff, more like), hair plastered down with

Brylcream, "Do you come here often ?" was about the pinnacle of my chat up lines at that time, though I probably improved with practice. That, of course, was when a girl accepted your invitation to take a whirl of the dance floor. Sometimes one was rude enough to decline, leaving you to walk back to where you came from, publicly humiliated, and dead scared to try with a different girl in case she found you equally unattractive. I know, 'cos I've been there.

Advancing teenage years and approaching physical maturity gradually changed all that and quite a collection of amenable young ladies was accumulated. What a thrill to find that when the music struck up one of them was actually looking at YOU, smiling and visibly willing you to ask her. Then it was merely a case of smiling back and inclining your head towards the dance floor and she'd meet you half way.

It was at two such dances, one on Saturday night at Stoney Lane Barracks and Moseley and Balsall Heath Institute on the Monday night that I found myself the target of a gang of Irish youths...and Tony paid the price!

As the Saturday night dance came to end a brawl suddenly erupted near the exit. I hadn't a clue what it was about or who was involved but it became like one huge rugby scrum with lots of girls screaming and blokes shouting and throwing punches. In the thick of it I noticed that a small dark-haired girl who was a regular at the dance, but who I didn't know, had got knocked to the ground and was in danger of being severely trampled on by the mob around her.

To avoid her being perhaps seriously injured I pushed my way through the jostling bodies and helped her to get up to her feet and scramble clear, escorted her to the door, and off we went our separate ways.

I was in the RAF, at Church Lawford at the time and Tony had been demobbed.

To get there on a Monday night I had to hitch-hike home along the A45 by thumbing down long-distance lorries. It was easy in those days if you were in uniform, about one in five would stop, probably ex-servicemen, so it was a regular Monday night jaunt of mine.

To get back to camp I used to take a 'bus to the Swan pub at Yardley where I knew a Birmingham Gazette newspaper delivery van, driven by a neighbour at 21 Ansell Road named Jimmy, would pick me up and take me at some speed to the top of the lane to the camp near Rugby, which was on his route, opposite a well-known drivers' all-night café called the Blue Boar.

This Monday night was different, though. The dance had not been on long when the gang of Irishmen, from the slums of Dublin I suspect, in Birmingham as road work labourers, filed in and formed a group of about ten, opposite where our party always stood. After one dance I was walking off the floor when suddenly I was surrounded by the Irish gang. Their intention was obvious. I was to suffer for having rescued the girl and, I guess, in their eyes, having interfered in their affairs. Perhaps the Saturday night fight had been over her. I'll never know.

Anyway, just as you see in films, everyone scattered leaving me isolated in the middle of the circle...except Tony, who come and stood by my side. I shouted out for someone to 'phone the police but I couldn't see that anyone did. To distract the gang I ran swiftly towards the exit door where there was a secretary's office, expecting some of the gang to follow me – it was me they wanted, after all - but banking on getting to the safety of the office and 'phoning for the police.

I gate-crashed into the office, looking and sounding fraught, probably wild-eyed, as though being pursued by the hounds of the Baskervilles, to be confronted by a large table with people sitting around it, obviously holding a committee meeting. Incensed by my unseemly entrance, they started ordering me out as I pleaded with them to call the police because there was serious trouble in the dance hall and my brother was at risk.

All this took only a few seconds but when I got back into the hall each of Tony's arms was being held back by one of the Irishman. Another had his thick leather belt from his trousers raised in threatening fashion. Before I could get to him to grab his arm he swung the belt at my brother's face. Tony turned it to his right-hand side to protect his eyes and the buckle of the belt opened up a nasty gash beneath his left eye. He still had this scar well into old age. And he hadn't done a darn thing except, as always, try to protect me.

As for the cowardly assailants, they disappeared into the night air and I went with Tony on the 'bus to hospital to have his wound stitched before walking home. I then had to hitch-hike back to my RAF camp 30 miles away to be on duty at crack of dawn next day. Weren't exactly cosseted with attention in those days, were we ?

Chapter 12
'...you were bawled at, goaded, insulted, belittled and driven to extremes of physical effort'

Within some eight years of the war being over, and while the cold war with Russia was still very much in place, first Tony (1948/1950) and then I (1951-53) had to undertake our two years of National Service...hence two more of Ma Shaw's brood being prepared for possible action, this time with possible nuclear overtones.

We both served in the Royal Air Force, on the clerical side, Tony stationed near Gloucester while I was at RAF Church Lawford, an airfield construction depot, near Rugby, after eight-weeks intensive 'square-bashing' training at RAF Weeton, Blackpool.

Square-Bashing! That, believe me, in those years when the world could quite easily have been plunged into nuclear conflict, gave a whole new perspective to the word 'discipline'. It had to be so because Britain was in an underlying but constant state of high alert. It wasn't going to be almost caught napping again, as had been the case in the build up to to WW2.

Those eight weeks of marching on the parade ground, receiving weapon training and generally being knocked into shape by Drill Instructors (DI s) ensured that a huge reservoir of well-trained young men was in reserve. Just in case...

Did I say 'knocked into shape'? From the moment you tumbled out of the truck (or 'garry' I think it was called) that transported you from the kitting-out station (with a uniform that didn't fit!) at Padgate to your square-bashing camp you were bawled at, goaded, insulted, belittled and driven to extremes of physical effort that you didn't realise you possessed. Here again -at the risk of sounding boring and repetitive – I was better prepared than most because Tony had already been through the mill, at RAF Bridgnorth, and had given me due warning.

It was late August to early September in a very hot summer. You paraded in the heat of the day in thick uniform, wearing heavy boots and tight-fitting beret while carrying out rifle drills, again and again and again. The sweat would pour down your neck and from under your arms, the wasps would crawl down your nose as the DI snarled order after order at you. If you dared to flap the wasp away from your face you we humiliated yet again by the DI s verbal disdain.

They had a language all of their own, too. It was though it was 'poncy' to say words as they were meant to be said. So as you marched they chanted 'YEFT...YEFT...YEFT-YOIGHT -YEFT...'. And other strange commands that I can't recall. Then it was time for a change: march at the double back to your hut and change into weapon-training gear in three or four minutes, leaving your bedside area all neat and tidy with nothing on display. Then, at the double, dash off to learn how to fire rifles, climb over a Jacob's Ladder, crawl through the undergrowth without being seen. Then do it all again, hour after hour, day after day.

As a background to all this, the tidiness with which we had to keep our huts, each housing 32 airmen with a corporal in charge, was at roughly the level of that required for a State Visit to Windsor Castle. We had a piece of cord the length of the billet. With this we lined up the 16 beds on each side.

Before beginning our duties each day, our bedclothes had to be folded into what were known as 'biscuits'. Each item of bed clothing was folded down to about one yard in width. They were then stacked blanket, sheet, blanket, blanket, sheet, blanket, and then bound around with another blanket. These neat piles were placed at the head of each bed and then lined up with the aid of the length of cord. Our white towel, which must never show any sign of having been used, was folded across the centre of the bed...and all lined up with the cord.

On the centre of the towel was your mug, as clean and shiny as the days it was made, and 'irons' namely knife fork and spoon, clean and shiny as new. These were , of course, all lined up with our precious length of cord. At the side of each bed was a small locker to display brushes, polish tins and the like and all had to be spotless at all times, even when you had just used them. We used to use a razor blade to scrape off any stray polish marks after we had finished using them.

In the centre aisle of the billet there were two cylindrical, iron, coke-burning fires with a chimney pipe up through the ceiling and roof to take the smoke and fumes away. Beside the fire was a large, deep, oblong iron coke holder. Obviously, during the hot summer while we were there they were never in use so they had to be kept black-lead polished at all times, even the inside of the coke holder.

Our boots, despite being used to pound the parade ground for hours each day, had to be as shiny as if to be worn by Coldstream Guards on Queen's Birthday parade. Each night we dutifully polished the toe caps, spit on top of the polish, massaged it in with small circular movements, then added more spit and more polish until they shone like the panel work of a Rolls Royce. Then you went out marching again the next day, inevitably causing a web of cracks in your good work, and so repaired the damage again the next night.

Talking of shiny surfaces the floor of the billet had to be as near to doubling up as a looking glass as we could get it. This was achieved by conventional sweeping and polish but then came our big secret....at the door of the billet at each end were piles of twelve-inch square pieces of felt. These were used as footpads so that footwear was removed on entry before skating around the billet at all times, polishing as you went. And woe betide any foolish sprog who moved around without felt beneath his feet. As if this wasn't enough domestic drudgery, there was one night each week set aside as 'Bull Night' when you collectively cleaned the billet, including all those windows, from top to bottom.

From the demands of this regime there was no escape, and nor was there meant to be. While you were out during the day, there would be random NCO's inspections of each billet. If a mug was seen to have been used and not thoroughly cleaned afterwards it would be on the floor, smashed when you returned. Yet the contradiction to all this way-over-the-top cleanliness was that the outside toilet block was hardly ever cleaned and it was always cold water that came out of the so-called hot water taps.

Same with the showers and the bath, though nobody used it: no hot water. I was at Weeton during the very hot weather so I could get by with washing, shaving and showering with cold water. Shaving must have been a real problem to those with dark, heavy beards. I was fair-haired and with not much of a growth when I was eighteen so it was never a problem to me.

I do recall quite vividly, when we first arrived, watching a squad of recruits who were obviously just about to undertake passing out parade, having completed their eight weeks. At that time our group clumped along, out of step much of the time, looking ill-fitted-out in our new uniforms and hats. The word 'SPROGS', personified.

"You're a nasty little sprog, Shaw....what are you?".... "I'm a nasty little sprog..." ..."Yes, and you're a nasty little sprog WHAT, Shaw?" ..."I''m a nasty little sprog, CORPORAL...".." That's better you nasty little sprog..." This was the kind of exchange that took place early in those eight weeks as the DI s set about turning squads of bemused and baffled boys into possibly a confident fighting force of well-trained men.

Watching that squad of new airmen, of just eight weeks experience, yeft-yoighting along the tarmac road, thirty-two sets of heels striking the ground in harmony, with just one click, shoulders back, chest out, stomach sucked in, arms swinging in unison to the level of his waist belt, forward swing and back swing, made you hope, with a sense of awe, that you could possibly be like that in eight weeks time. And we were... fit, smart, more confident and well capable of looking after ourselves.

At that point some of the DI s actually smiled, shook our hands and wished us luck. They'd done their job and done it well...the boys of No.8 Flight, 'B' Squadron, No.9. School of Recruit Training, RAF Weeton had passed out as full-blown airmen. Now the Drill Instructors could be human again. Until the next truckload of sprogs rolled in.

Chapter 13
'...I decided I could take liberties'

Audrey Taylor's parents' recognition of her as being worthy of further education when she left school took her to Secretarial College in the centre of Birmingham, the acquisition of good grades in shorthand and typing and, via one short-term job, a position in the commercial/advertising department of the Birmingham Gazette and Despatch.

To be able to afford it her parents used the newly-introduced 'Child Allowance' to pay, or part pay, for the further education that elevated her from the likely shop assistant or whatever career that, with no other qualifications, she might have become, to a far more interesting one...and here we go again with that word 'fate', though I still don't believe it.

I can remember, if not the first time I saw her, then certainly one of the first times. She had just started in what we editorial people called 'the front office'. She was attractive, wearing what I thought of as a 'cowboy' style brown check shirt/blouse. She was slim, nice legs in high-heel shoes, light-brown almost shoulder-length hair. We talked easily, she liked football, her dad and her brother, Stan, used to take her to Birmingham City matches.

She was interested in my job as a would-be football reporter and that helped the conversation no end. Most girls at the time thought that football came second only to war films as men's most boring topic of conversation. Audrey was different. She liked chatting to the men around the workplace and not just to be flirty, (though she was just a bit) because she was comfortable and relaxed in male company.

One thing she told me, for instance, was how when her dad was on duty on a Blues home game Saturdays it meant he was doing the Lickey Banker run. This was a goods train that had to pull its wagons on an upward sloping stretch of line that went near the Lickey Hills and passed alongside the St Andrews.

On heavy, damp days in the winter he would build up a head of steam as he approached St Andrews and then toot his whistle and release it as he passed the ground, sending a cloud of thick smoke across the pitch, hanging low in the heavy conditions. This was before the Railway End Stand was built so there was no obstruction to stop the smoke and steam swirling among the players, which it did, quite often.

Not long after she had come to work at the Gazette I went off to do my National Service and, one Saturday, I went into the newspaper office, on the corner of Dalton Street and Newton Street, though the 'front office' was in Corporation Street almost opposite the Birmingham Law Courts. Who should be in the lobby by the lift but...well, you've guessed. She was glammed up, looking good, small suitcase at her feet. She was about to catch a train nearby, off on holidays and so I insisted on taking her to the station. How the heck could she carry a suitcase wearing heels like THAT !

When I came out of the RAF she had been promoted to secretary to the Circulation Manager and her office was... wait for it...dead opposite that of the Sporting Buff, where I worked. At that point 'coincidences' cropped up thick and fast. It seemed as though each time I left the office, (at the same time each day) to fetch a tray of tea from the canteen, her office door would open. She was off to the canteen with a tray of tea cups as well.

At that time there was a free lunchtime dance at the old Casino Ballroom, about a hundred yards from the Gazette/ Despatch offices. She would go there for an hour. So would I. Surprise, surprise, sometimes we would dance together. By then, with two years in the RAF behind me, I'd progressed beyond the 'Do you come here often?' chatline. Now it was probably more like : "I see your team lost again on Saturday...". What a charmer, eh?

Then one Sunday morning when I turned up to catch the office transit van with the rest of the football team, to play a match in the Festival League, Audrey and two of her pals, Mary and Varna, turned up as well.

In contrast to when she went off on holiday Audrey wasn't glammed up at all this time. Dumbed down, in fact. She wore a dreadful pair of purple trousers and that was the catalyst for what happened on the return journey, with two young women jostling about in the back with a dozen or so blokes, all standing up in a rickety newspaper van, clattering along. It was because she was wearing trousers, and not a skirt or frock, as most girls did in those days, I decided I could take liberties.

I trapped her in the corner of the van, picked her up, turned her upside down, held her by her heels and said:"Will you come to the pictures with me tomorrow night?" before putting her back on her feet again."I thought you'd never ask," she replied, or words to that effect. We went to see *Affair with a Stranger* at the Gaumont Cinema in Steelhouse Lane Birmingham on October 12 1953 and the following Sunday we went to see *The Eddie Cantor Story* at the Bristol Cinema on Bristol Road.

And, yes I do remember it well...

It was the start of what, at the time of writing, has been a 58-year relationship. In the weeks and months that followed we became best friends long, long before we became lovers. We were married on July 7, 1956 and she's been a terrific asset to me in always understanding my unsociable working hours, never whinging when she had to hang about waiting for me for hours, enjoying all the of the sport-based functions we've attended and solidly supporting everything I've ever done.

The year after we were married included an episode in my professional life that has never been bettered, before or since. Those earlier, pre-call up days of taking the telephone to either Villa Park or St Andrews in order to telephone the report written by the Sports Argus writers of the day including Charlie 'Mac' Matheson, Doug Norman, Dick Knight and others, had been very beneficial because soon I was invited to be the reporter rather than the messenger.

Then, before the start of the 1957 FA Cup campaign, the Argus Editor, Ron Haines, told us that we were each to get a team for the third round and we would stay with that team until they were knocked out. Aston Villa being the least likely of the West Midland teams to make progress, (they were away to a very strong Luton Town team at the first hurdle) they would be 'my' team.

History tells what happened then....Villa reached the FA Cup Final for the first time since 1924 (when they lost) and were playing the fabulous pre-Munich Manchester United Matt Busby Babes at Wembley. So, just like having been thought to have 'no chance' of getting to Wembley at all, they had 'no chance' of winning the Cup. But they did, for the first time since 1920 and, currently, they haven't won it since. If anyone cares to dig deep and find the Sports Argus for Saturday May 5, 1957, they will find that young Dennis, the blitz kid, wrote the running report.

Another lucky turn of events led, some 35 years or so later, to my unexpectedly enjoying another Wembley Stadium experience that is actually lasting quite a long while. At the time, in the early 1990s, one of my jobs as a freelance journalist, was to write a lot of material for Aston Villa FC, including some of their match-day programme editorial and commercial brochures.

The commercial manager for a spell was Tony Stephens (later to become a leading football agent) who left to become, quite briefly, chief executive of Wembley Stadium. Soon he was on the telephone to me asking if I would write a commercial brochure for Wembley Stadium similar to one I had written for Aston Villa, basically explaining all of their activities outside of staging football matches.

Later I had a call from Stephens to say that his board were pleased with the text for the brochure and they particularly liked a phrase that I had used in one section referring to Wembley as 'this Venue of Legends'. It seems they had been attempting, without success, to dream up a slogan for the Stadium and that 'The Venue of Legends' was just what they were after. To my surprise, when the old Wembley was replaced by the new, they still called it The Venue of Legends on their website. What a shame it doesn't pay royalties...!

Looking back to my dad and brothers telling me, when I was about six years old, about such topics as Aston Villa, the pink Saturday night sports paper and the wonders of Wembley Stadium I'll admit to having felt unbelievably fortunate that sheer chance had enabled me to make a little tiny mark on each of them. (No, let's be honest: I'm well chuffed...!)

And so, in the half-a-century and more of happy family life that has followed there have been many, many memorable celebratory gatherings some of them mercifully in the early days of our marriage before Ma Shaw died and I like to think that she saw enough of how we all strove to follow the ideals that she and dad had instilled in us to believe that her lifetime of struggles had been worthwhile.

One of them, long after she had died, sticks in mind for one of those story-lines that you can see on TV soap operas and not quite believe. We were celebrating my 65th birthday in 1998 with a gathering of relatives and friends at an apartment owned by brother Jim in Mudeford, overlooking the wonderful Christchurch Harbour. While explaining to Tony's third wife, Pauline, the details of how the jig-saw of our mystifying family fitted together Jim overheard, nudged me, inclined his head towards the kitchen, and beckoned me to follow him.

Once out of earshot of the others he said; "I'm sorry but you've got that wrong, Dennis. I'm illegitimate..."

Without over-dramatising my reaction, it's true to say that for a moment or two I was paralysed and incapable of speaking. That word 'illegitimate' sounded so ghastly. It has no meaning now in terms of a person's status in life but it had in days gone by. Young women who had children out of wedlock, especially young Roman Catholic women, were regarded as having brought shame on the hypocrites who condemned them. (How different in the aftermath of WW2. By the 21st century there were probably more babies born out of wedlock than in, and supported by the welfare system)

Jim went on to explain that if you look at his birth certificate you'll see he was born in 1919. Mom's husband was killed in 1915. Jim's father was the soldier who bought her husband's belongings back home from the battlefield. Jack Potter. They started a relationship after what must have been a tearful first meeting. She thought it would lead to marriage but when she discovered she was pregnant he informed her he was already married.

It would be impossible to explain how I felt about it. Appalled to think that my mom, the lady who throughout my life had always been nearer to Mother Theresa than someone who could be used as Jack Potter used her. I was angry that for all those years I hadn't been told. Desperately, desperately sad at the mental turmoil mom must have gone through, at probably being condemned by people who weren't fit to breathe the same air as her.

And then there was Jim. Why should he call himself 'illegitimate'. He was a bloody hero, for heaven's sake, a role model, an ex-soldier who had helped to save us, you and I, from the ' monstrous tyranny' that Winston Churchill described.

My emotions were stirred up by the news, still are, but Jim was unmoved. Frank Shaw was his dad, the one who was there from the time he was old enough to remember. Frank Shaw gave him advice on just about everything he needed... don't buy a bike on hire purchase my son. Be patient, save a few more months and pay cash. Never spend all your wages every week. Always put a little by and your savings will build up. "I'll never forget all the sound advice that dad gave me, " Jim told me, and he didn't mean Jack Potter. He meant OUR dad, the one who joined with our mom, and made us a proper family.

Chapter 14.

'...I would have imagined our mom, as if in some great musical hall in the sky'

In July 2009 Normandy veteran Jim, who has two grandsons Andrew and Peers, celebrated his 90th birthday at the Harbour Heights Hotel Restaurant, overlooking Sandbanks and Poole Harbour, near where his delightful partner Peggy and he live in a smart apartment with necessary services for the elderly constantly on hand.

Among the party around the table were his two sons Keith and Carl, Tony and Pauline and myself, plus one of Jim's closest mates, a fellow war veteran from the Normandy campaign who was turned ninety and still sprightly. Jim and Peg became ideal companions in the latter years after their respective spouses had died, Peg being the widow of one of Jim's late professional colleagues.

After the war, while still in the Army, Jim had set about getting himself educated up to the necessary standard to move into what was then 'Personnel' work, later to be Human Resources and he advanced quickly. From the post of assistant personnel manager at Bird's Custard works Digbeth, Birmingham, he was head-hunted to help to set up Campbell Soups' new factory in King's Lynn and was subsequently head-hunted again to do a similar job for General Foods in Banbury, where he completed a distinguished career.

While living in the Banbury vicinity he was presented with a Queen's Silver Jubilee Award for his services to British Industry and was chairman of the Anglo-American Relations Board, working to this end with the Brize Norton US air base. As he moves toward his 92nd birthday it seems clear that there's a longevity gene somewhere in the confusing mix of our ancestry. Florry and Ivy both lived past their 90th birthday while Tony celebrated his 80th in December 2010, though sadly only one of his two sons, David was there. The other one, Tim, had died suddenly of a heart attack in 2003.

Having become an octogenarian, Tony was still responsible for the long-lasting fund-raising, match-day draw scheme at Crystal Palace Football Club, for whom he was commercial manager when Terry Venables was creating what became known as 'the team of the eighties'. After Tony finished his national service he wanted more than hanging around the advertisement department of the Birmingham Mail and set off on new career that eventually took him into football.

From Crystal Palace he went on to become chief executive and a director of Millwall , chief executive of Charlton Athletic, and chairman of the Football League Commercial Managers' Association. When the Football League Executive Staff Association was born he was the commercial committee representative who served on FA Disciplinary meetings and others to decide transfer fees.

All this and, after having not gone into athletics seriously until he was demobbed, and having not starting training in earnest until he was turned 20, he became captain of Birchfield Harriers, won several AAA championship relay medals with a trio of Olympics runners as team mates (Peter Radford, Mike Rawson and Johnny Salisbury) and was one of the 'possibles' for 200 metres in the 1956 Olympics Melbourne (though, realistically, he was never going to make the team).

Currently Jim, Tony and I remain of some dozen or so children that mom and dad reared either permanently, as their own, or took under their wing when some might otherwise have been homeless. That includes a young girl not previously mentioned named Marion, whom I know little about, but who they took in for quite a lengthy spell during the 1930s, when she would otherwise have had nowhere to go.

As their descendants we have striven, sometimes against the odds, to continue a 'family first' culture which, nationally, has sadly appeared to be more and more in terminal decline with co-habitation taking over from marriage and more and more children being reared as 'single parent' families. Audrey and I celebrated our Golden Wedding at Maxstoke Park Golf Club in July 2006, attended, along with a circle of friends, by our sons and their wives Mark and Jo and Steve and Sue and our daughters and their husbands Joanne and Steve and Donna and James. There, too, were our grandchildren Claire & Gary, Holly, Katie and Lucy, Laura and Karl, and Natalie. We now also have great grandchildren Chloe, Dyon and Kacey.

If I were a 'believer' I would have imagined our mom, as if in some great musical hall in the sky, putting on dad's bowler, picking up a walking stick, conjuring that soft little smile and singing just one more time: "I'm going back to the shack where the black-eyed Susan's grow"...because you can be sure she would have done, if only she could.

END

EPILOGUE

Our Mom is a tree now. Or, to put it more accurately, there is a tree growing robustly in her memory. Her surviving sons and daughters arranged to have one planted in her name at the National Memorial Arboretum, Alrewas, between Lichfield and Burton-on Trent, just off the A38.

I like that, because it seems so appropriate, as though she has roots going down into the earth, ever deeper, while, above ground a tree will continue to grow upwards and outwards in her name for many years to come, a century or more, almost as though a part of her lives on.

When she died, in Little Bromwich Hospital, Birmingham on September 22, 1974. aged 81 , she had carefully upgraded her insurance life policy along the way, in step with inflation, so that there was enough to pay for her funeral. She must have kept in touch with the going rate in order not to be a drain on her family when her time was up and that, perhaps, summed up Ma Shaw..

For the first two years of our married life (from 1956 to 1958), Audrey and I lived with her in 21 Ansell Road. Our bedroom was the one that had been so severely cracked during the blitz but it must have been repaired by then. When we moved out our mom, independent to the last, elected to move to an old folks bungalow in Chelmsley Wood, not far from where Florry then lived in a tower block. From those far off 'hilarious' days of 12 around the dinner table she was now on her own, but she was visited by family fairly regularly, so I think she was contented enough.

She was buried without a headstone and I personally had no feelings about that at the time. I don't visit graves, myself. I never think of people I've cared for rotting away underground. But a tree ! That's something different entirely. The National Memorial Arboretum is part of the National

Forest, bequeathed to the nation to mark the millennium and is transforming 200 square miles of Central England. Already nearly eight million trees have been planted across Staffordshire, Leicestershire and Nottinghamshire, thereby increasing woodland cover from 6% to 18%.

In the Arboretum part of it, mom's tree is surrounded by other such trees in memory mostly of service personnel who have been killed in many conflicts around the world. She was not, of course, killed in conflict but she did suffer all the agonies associated with losing loved ones in heart-rending fashion as chronicled in these pages. Let's be honest, fighting wars is mostly about men – blokes doing blokey things – though more women have become warriors from approaching the 21st century and beyond. Looking back to WW1 and WW2 while many brave women served their country, the mothers, the wives, girl friends, daughters were left behind, to just get on with it.

A comparatively small number were forced to battle on, day-by-day on the Home Front in not one, but two world wars, taking on board indignity after indignity, pain after pain, heartbreak after heartbreak, taken for granted pretty much. I hope these pages are a reminder to us all, of the part these ladies, like Our Mom, played in keeping the Home Fires burning.

> Keep the home fires burning,
> While your hearts are yearning
> Though the lads are far away
> They dream of home
> There's a silver lining
> Through the dark clouds shining
> Turn the dark clouds inside out
> Till the boys come home

* One verse of the WW1 song by Ivor Novello

Lightning Source UK Ltd.
Milton Keynes UK

178179UK00009B/24/P